The
Faith
to
Flourish

The
Faith
to
Flourish

*God's design for a rooted,
resilient, and fruitful life*

Christine Caine

NELSON
BOOKS

An Imprint of Thomas Nelson

The Faith to Flourish

Published by Nelson Books, an imprint of Thomas Nelson, 501 Nelson Place, Nashville, TN 37214, USA. Nelson Books and Thomas Nelson are registered trademarks of HarperCollins Christian Publishing, Inc.

Published in association with Yates & Yates, www.yates2.com.

Thomas Nelson titles may be purchased in bulk for educational, business, fundraising, or sales promotional use. For information, please email SpecialMarkets@ThomasNelson.com.

Unless otherwise noted, Scripture quotations are taken from the Christian Standard Bible®, Copyright © 2017 by Holman Bible Publishers. Used by permission. Christian Standard Bible® and CSB®, are federally registered trademarks of Holman Bible Publishers. Scripture quotations marked AMPC are taken from the Amplified® Bible (AMPC). Copyright © 1954, 1958, 1962, 1964, 1965, 1987 by The Lockman Foundation. Used by permission. www.lockman. org. Scripture quotations marked ESV are taken from the ESV® Bible (The Holy Bible, English Standard Version®). Copyright © 2001 by Crossway, a publishing ministry of Good News Publishers. All rights reserved. Scripture quotations marked NASB1995 are taken from the New American Standard Bible®. Copyright © 1960, 1971, 1977, 1995 by The Lockman Foundation. Used by permission. All rights reserved. www.lockman.org. Scripture quotations marked NET are taken from the NET Bible® copyright ©1996–2017 by Biblical Studies Press, L.L.C. http://netbible.com All rights reserved. Scripture quotations marked NKJV are taken from the New King James Version®. Copyright © 1982 by Thomas Nelson. Used by permission. All rights reserved. Scripture quotations marked NLT are taken from the Holy Bible, New Living Translation. © 1996, 2004, 2015 by Tyndale House Foundation. Used by permission of Tyndale House Publishers, Inc., Carol Stream, Illinois 60188. All rights reserved.

All emphasis in Scripture quotations is added by the author.

Any internet addresses, phone numbers, or company or product information printed in this book are offered as a resource and are not intended in any way to be or to imply an endorsement by Thomas Nelson, nor does Thomas Nelson vouch for the existence, content, or services of these sites, phone numbers, companies, or products beyond the life of this book.

HarperCollins Publishers, Macken House, 39/40 Mayor Street Upper, Dublin 1, D01 C9W8, Ireland (https://www.harpercollins.com)

Library of Congress Cataloging-in-Publication Data

Names: Caine, Christine author
Title: The faith to flourish : God's design for a rooted, resilient, and fruitful life / by Christine Caine.
Description: Nashville, TN : Nelson Books, [2026] | Summary: "Discover the resilience, peace, and purpose you can cultivate through the symbolism of the olive tree, as Christine Caine reveals how to flourish even in the face of life's darkest times"-- Provided by publisher.
Identifiers: LCCN 2025014447 (print) | LCCN 2025014448 (ebook) | ISBN 9781400255252 hardcover | ISBN 9781400255375 ebook
Subjects: LCSH: Christian life--Biblical teaching | Olive in the Bible
Classification: LCC BS680.C47 C35 2026 (print) | LCC BS680.C47 (ebook) | DDC 248.4--dc23/eng/20250922
LC record available at https://lccn.loc.gov/2025014447
LC ebook record available at https://lccn.loc.gov/2025014448

To my beloved olive shoots, Catherine and Sophia.

Blessed is everyone who fears the LORD,
who walks in his ways! . . .
Your children will be like olive shoots
around your table.
PSALM 128:1, 3 ESV

Contents

Introduction

The Sacred Olive Tree

But I am like a flourishing olive tree
in the house of God;
I trust in God's faithful love forever and ever.
PSALM 52:8

Standing in the ruins of the sanctuary Pandrosos high atop the Acropolis, where I'd taken a group of friends to see the Parthenon, I did my best to listen to our tour guide. Having hiked the gravel paths to the top of the mount numerous times since my first trip in 1987 and starting to tire from the summer heat, I was definitely beginning to fade. Still, being Greek and being in Greece, I wanted my friends to experience the most Greek thing Greece has going—the Parthenon.

Growing up in a big, crazy Greek family, we had images of the Parthenon throughout our home. I daresay my mum had a replica of it on the end of the mantel that never moved, not even when baby Jesus and the entire Nativity set was brought out at

Christmas and sprawled across the remaining space. Of course, I would choose Jesus over the Parthenon any day, but back then, as a child, I never would have suggested we move Mum's replica or any of the other Greek trinkets scattered throughout our house, which all paid homage to the homeland and its ancient treasures.

Designed twenty-five centuries ago, the Parthenon stands tall against a sky that's often as blue as the Greek flag or the Aegean Sea—both of which are breathtaking to me. Though constructed between 447 and 438 BC as a celebration for the Hellenic victory over Persian invaders during the Greco-Persian Wars, the Parthenon has always served as a temple dedicated to the goddess Athena Parthenos—the namesake for the city of Athens.[1] Architects around the world have called the Parthenon the most beautiful building ever built.[2] Though it survived the first six hundred years in its original state, it went on to see years of conquests, bombings, reconstructions, and preservation work.[3]

But none of its classical architecture captured my attention that day. What left me in awe was a lone olive tree standing in the midst of sand-colored rock. While my friends had been listening more intently to the tour guide, I had wandered a little and happened upon the tree.

A nearby information plaque labeled it "The Sacred Olive Tree." As legend has it, every tree that has stood in that exact location can be traced to the original tree—the one believed to have been planted more than twenty-five hundred years ago and, according to Greek mythology, a gift from the goddess Athena herself. As folklore has it, when Athena and Poseidon competed for the patronage of the city, she struck the ground with her spear, and the initial sprig of the olive tree sprouted.[4] Of course, actual history has a much different account, with the most recent planting being placed there by the American School of Archeology in 1952, after they saved and harvested a four-foot branch from the previous tree that endured the destruction of World War II.[5]

Whatever its beginning, from my perspective The Sacred Olive Tree deserved to be revered. Its existence in such a place was as astonishing as the Parthenon itself. What resilience. What strength. What extraordinary ability to not only survive and grow but thrive and flourish. All alone. Atop the highest point in Athens. No wonder that, for centuries, The Sacred Olive Tree has remained a worthy symbol of the city and an undying and ancient representation of peace, hope, abundance, and resurrection.[6]

And yet, despite all that, I had never really noticed it. Later, on the journey home, I found myself thinking of nothing else, and the more I thought about The Sacred Olive Tree, the more curious I became about olive trees everywhere.

Soon it seemed that every time I opened my Bible, there was a mention of an olive tree or an olive or olive oil. I realized God may have been trying to get my attention, so I decided to do a deep dive into all things olive tree in Scripture, and I was astounded by all I discovered. Through extensive study and research, I found that olive trees are depicted as a symbol of life, as productivity, fruitfulness, beauty, and dignity. They are depicted as an essential source of food, lamp oil, anointing oil, sacrificial oil, medicine, and wood for furniture. What's more, when Jesus prayed before he went to the cross, it was on the Mount of Olives in the Garden of Gethsemane. He prayed in the middle of an olive grove! And when the Holy Spirit came as Jesus promised, it was olive oil that became symbolic of his anointing. Yes, I had read these accounts so many times, but I never knew the significance of the olive tree in those passages. I never knew that Scripture mentions olive trees, olives, olive wood, olive branches, and olive oil more than two hundred times. I had been reading the Bible for almost four decades, and yet somehow I had missed so much.

The passage that captured my attention and heart during my research process is from Psalm 52. David wrote this powerful psalm when he was on the run and being slandered, lied about, mocked, and laughed at. He was hiding in caves because Saul wanted to kill him. He was alone, exhausted, confused, and ridiculed, yet he wrote, "But I am like a flourishing olive tree in the house of God; I trust in God's faithful love forever and ever."[7] Another translation says, "a green olive tree," and *green* means "flourishing."[8]

I kept coming back to this verse because I could not understand how you could be attacked, persecuted, feel isolated, run for your life, and simultaneously declare that you are like a flourishing olive tree. David seemed to be saying that we can thrive in life even if our circumstances are challenging, our relationships are strained, our dreams have been shattered, or we are being shamed, slandered, or persecuted. That sounded like real life to me, and I was intrigued by David's tenacity, strength, courage, and resilience in the midst of chaos, confusion, pain, and disappointment. Was it really possible to flourish despite external circumstances? That question sparked the idea for this book.

I understand that we may never find ourselves running for our lives the way David did, but there is no doubt that every one of us has experienced times of disappointment, disillusionment, discouragement, betrayal, loss, grief, false accusation, misunderstanding, or traumatic seasons of pain and suffering—be it mentally, emotionally, or physically. Such pain leaves us feeling demoralized, deflated, and depleted, doesn't it? But from what David declared, if we are found in Christ, then we can be in the *midst* of chaos without being in *inner* chaos.

When David said he was a green flourishing olive tree in the house of the Lord, his deliverance was still in the future. But he was so confident that it was coming, he was already singing about how thankful he was going to be. He knew God would deliver him in time because he had done it before. What a reminder for us all: God is with us; God is for us; and God has gone before us.

Wanting to learn all I could about olive trees, I broadened my research to include dendrology—the study of trees—historical information, and even trips to olive farms. It became my routine, as I traveled in my work, to look for olive farms anywhere nearby to visit. So many times, when I'd be standing in the middle of a grove of olive trees, I couldn't help but think of my mum and her obsession with olives and olive oil. She would have been so proud to know I was finally interested in what she considered the most important tree on earth and that I was learning what she was convinced of all along—everything goes back to the Greeks! This is why, in all my travels, I sought to settle once and for all the origin of olive trees, and I secretly hoped they really did originate in Greece like Mum believed. (Of course, that's what I'll always believe, too, but no doubt the Spaniards and the Italians will argue the point.)

More importantly, I found that though not very tall or stately, olive trees are very long-lasting, dependable, and resilient. They display permanence and endurance, sometimes living for thousands of years. They can thrive in the worst of conditions.

I learned about their fruit, the products made from the wood, their enemies, their medicinal properties, and how to grow and care for them.

I was continually amazed by how much olive trees had permeated different aspects of our lives. Did you know there is a World Olive Tree Day? It takes place November 26. Who knew? And did you know that olive trees have been depicted in art throughout history? They've been the subjects of Claude Monet, Henri Matisse, and Salvador Dali. One of my favorite works of art is *Olive Grove*, which is part of a series of olive tree paintings from 1889 by Van Gogh.[9]

I also found the mention of olive trees in poetry, songs, movies, and historical writings. In *The Odyssey*, an ancient poem attributed to Homer, the description of two olive trees is used to convey a sense of reassurance, letting the reader know of the legendary Greek King Odysseus's safety.[10] I found songs from the sixties and films about justice and political issues using the olive tree as symbolism throughout. I even found a made-for-TV rom-com called *Love Under the Olive Tree* that's all about making olive oil. I'm not saying I watched it all the way through, but I was amazed at the ways olive trees have been depicted in the arts.

In the Nobel Prize Museum in Stockholm, the symbol of the olive branch represents the Nobel Peace Prize. The UN flag features the crown of olive branches circling the globe. The winners of the first ever Olympic games in Athens were rewarded with a crown of olive branches, and in 2004 at the Athens Olympic games, every champion wore a crown of olive branches to pay tribute to the Olympic spirit. From AD 797 to 802, Roman imperial coins featured the Empress Eirene. She was the personification of peace, and she held an olive branch upward in her right hand.

The use of olive branches as peace symbols has also been extended into treaties. The American Continental Congress originally drafted a document called the Olive Branch Petition to deliver to Great Britain in hopes of avoiding what became the Revolutionary War.[11] And Picasso's painting of a dove bearing an olive branch was used in the poster prepared for the first World Peace Congress held after World War II.

Even olive oil has its place on the world stage in history. In the pages of *The Iliad*, written in the eighth century BC, the Greek poet Homer referred to olive oil as "liquid gold."[12]

Mum never called it liquid gold, but she certainly treated it that way, and she raised me to love it—on everything. She understood that when you get to taste olive oil with a discerning palate, you only want more. I often joke, but I don't doubt it for a minute, that Mum put it in my baby bottle. After all, we were Greek! I love remembering all the ways my mother used olives and olive oil in everything we ate—and drank. I grew up with it as a staple in our kitchen and on our table, eating it on bread, and dousing it on cheese, salads, and sandwiches. You could say I was eating the Mediterranean Diet long before it was a thing. I remember Mum adding olive oil to recipes, rubbing it on her hands, and coating squeaky hinges with it. To Mum it was the cure-all and answer to everything. I feel sure her obsession with olive oil is why, to this day, I can't get enough of it. And I feel sure my love for olive trees began at a tender age, long before I laid eyes on The Sacred Olive Tree and began to understand the depth of their beauty and meaning.

I especially love olive trees when they are in full bloom and the sweet scent of the flowers fills a grove. I have two trees that grow in my front yard, and I get so happy each year when they begin to bud. Whether looking at them as I come and go in the driveway or when I plop a folding chair on the lawn and sit under them, they have a way of giving me life. I love to listen to the sound of the breeze rustling through the branches and causing the leaves to shimmer. I love watching the squirrels scamper up one side and down the other and then get into a game of chase. And when the trees start bearing fruit, I'm captivated by the idea that every flower did its best to produce an olive.

I'm excited to unpack the lessons I've learned from the olive tree, which I believe will help you to flourish spiritually, no matter what season of life you're in. In each lesson we'll explore a characteristic of the olive tree. We'll turn to Scripture to see how God wants that same quality to mature in us. And together we'll discover that every part of the olive tree is crucial from the root to the fruit—just like God never wastes any experience we live through on this earth. Every part of the olive tree offers us something to learn spiritually and then to weave practically into our lives for God's praise and his glory. I believe that by the time you read the last lesson, you'll be forever changed by the sacred olive tree.

LOVE,

Lesson 1

Root Yourself in God's Love

Not long ago, Nick and I got to hike one of the trails on my bucket list—the 7.5-mile Blue Trail that meanders through the five villages of Cinque Terre in Northern Italy. Full of twists and turns that hug seaside cliffs along the Mediterranean Sea, the trail is a marvel of engineering with breathtaking views. Some portions of our hike involved climbing up hewn steps carved out of the mountainside and carefully working our way down a steep and rocky hillside. At other times we traversed ancient stone footpaths or newly built ones made of wood jutting out over jagged rocks and crashing waves. For centuries the people in the nearby villages have farmed the terraced hillsides that line the trail. Each level features vegetable gardens, flower gardens, small vineyards, and—my favorite—olive trees.[1]

At one point I walked down the middle of a row of olive trees planted on either side of a stone path, and the canopy the trees made over the walkway felt like a cathedral—albeit not anywhere near that tall. Call it the romantic in me, but it was totally the perfect place for a wedding. But what impressed me more than all the picturesque beauty of the olive trees was how the trees clung to the side of the mountain. Despite the steep terraced hillside and winds from the sea, they were solidly anchored in place. That's because olive trees have robust root systems—ones that make them strong and enduring wherever they grow. They often live five hundred years but some are several thousand years old.[2]

Olive trees are known for having two kinds of roots with two specific purposes. First, a thick, strong taproot grows straight down and deep. Second, thinner shallow roots span out in every direction, going as far as twice the width of the canopy of the tree. The taproot is strong and anchors the tree to the earth, while the shallow roots running wide in the topsoil act as a stabilizing force. And both draw all the water and nutrients the tree needs to thrive. Because of this dual root system, olive trees can flourish in the driest of places. If the roots are well established, then they are resistant to drought and can go long periods of time, months even, without rain.[3]

The root system is so resilient that it's capable of regenerating itself even when the aboveground structure of the tree might be destroyed by frost, fire, or disease:

> In 1985, in Tuscany, a severe frost destroyed many productive and aged olive trees, ruining the livelihoods of farmers. However, new shoots appeared in the spring and when the dead wood was removed, the shoots became new fruit-producing trees.[4]

I saw a similar regeneration once while hiking the intense fifteen-mile trek up Santiago Peak, the highest mountain in the Santa Ana range in Orange County, California. Several months before, a huge fire had burned more than sixty acres, decimating part of the Cleveland National Forest. But on either side of the trail, new growth was appearing. It was evident that the forest floor, as well as all the undergrowth and towering trees, had been scorched black. Yet popping up everywhere were patches of wildflowers and green shoots—sprigs of ferns, grass, shrubs, and pine seedlings eager to become saplings now that they were no longer shaded by the towering canopies that once blanketed the top of the forest. It was so inspiring to see that nature wastes no time in making such a comeback, even after the most traumatic events—and it wouldn't be possible if all the plants and trees didn't have such strong roots running underground, still working to draw in nutrients and water to fuel such regrowth.

In the book of Job we read: "There is hope for a tree: If it is cut down, it will sprout again, and its shoots will not die. If its roots grow old in the ground and its stump starts to die in the soil, the scent of water makes it thrive and produce twigs like a sapling."[5] I love these verses because they give us hope for what seems hopeless in our lives. There is always the possibility of new life and the promise of resurrection.

> When we have strong roots—like the olive tree—we can keep growing, no matter what has left us disappointed, disillusioned, or utterly discouraged.

In the same way that the roots of grasses and ferns and trees can regenerate an entire forest, when we have strong spiritual roots that go deep in God, we can live a life of faith, endurance, perseverance, and resilience, moving forward through whatever life throws our way, bearing much fruit and fulfilling the plans and purpose God has for our lives. When we have strong roots—like the olive tree—we can keep growing, no matter what has left us disappointed, disillusioned, or utterly discouraged. No matter how much has burned to the ground and appears all but dead, there is always hope of new life.

The Start of Our New Life

Have you ever taken a cutting from a plant and rooted it? That's what it's called when you attempt to grow a new plant from a piece of another one. Typically, to root the cutting you place it in a small container filled with water and set it under a light—or where it can get plenty of sunshine. The objective is for it to absorb the water, sprout its first root, and then grow more roots. When it finally grows a healthy number of roots, you remove it from the container and plant it in soil—in the ground or in a pot. As it adapts to its new environment and anchors itself in the soil, it is considered to be rooted.[6]

To be rooted in something is to be "firmly implanted."[7] In our spiritual lives, once we become followers of Christ, we are rooted in Christ. When Paul wrote to the Colossians, he said, "So then, just as you have received Christ Jesus as Lord, continue to walk in him, being rooted and built up in him and established in the faith, just as you were taught, and overflowing with gratitude."[8]

That is such a powerful picture! In the Greek, *rooted* is *rhizoo,* an agricultural term that means being firmly established in the ground.[9] Being rooted, established, and built up, as Paul wrote, is something that happens *to* us. God roots us in him the moment we surrender our lives to the lordship of Christ, and then he continues to build us up.[10]

But the way we first become followers of Christ includes even more imagery. Paul wrote to the early Christians about how they were now a part of the family of God, and he added to our understanding the concept of grafting: "You, though a wild olive branch, were grafted in among them and have come to share in the rich root of the cultivated olive tree."[11]

I'll admit, when I first read this scripture many years ago, it left me utterly confused. I mean, I understand the idea of being rooted, but being grafted escaped me. Maybe you felt the same when you first read it. But over time I discovered that Paul used the metaphor of an olive tree—the emblematic perennial crop for many Mediterranean countries for more than six thousand years—to explain to the early Christians how they were made part of the family of God. What's more, Paul referenced both the wild olive tree and the cultivated olive tree—and the idea of one being grafted into the other. Even more interesting is that to this day "two taxonomic varieties are currently recognized: cultivated . . . and wild"—the same two Paul referenced.[12]

Before I explain the spiritual significance of all this, it's important to understand that in horticulture, grafting essentially takes two plants and fuses them together to become one. Together they can share the same rich roots and nutrients; together they can share the same sun, rain, and seasons. Together they can grow strong and bear fruit. Together they can become something they can't be apart. And this process of grafting has been practiced for centuries.

In biblical times the cultivated tree (the strong) was typically grafted into the wild tree (the weak).[13] But Paul reversed the natural order by saying that God took the wild olive tree (the weak) and grafted it into the cultivated tree (the strong). This is critical because before we were born again, we were like the wild olive trees (the weak), and now as followers of Christ we have been grafted into the cultivated tree (the strong), which is Jesus.

Basically, Paul was saying there is a spiritual grafting that brings us into the family of God and makes us heirs of the promises of God—regardless of our religious background, ethnicity, gender, social status, or anything else we might think would disqualify us. To explain this further, Galatians 3 tells us, "For through faith you are all sons of God in Christ Jesus. . . . And if you belong to Christ, then you are Abraham's seed, heirs according to the promise."[14] Through faith in Christ you and I are heirs to the promise God originally gave Abraham: "And I will make you a great nation. . . . And in you all the families of the earth will be blessed."[15] The nation of which Abraham was the father and through whom God chose to bless the earth was the nation of Israel—a people God chose to be his own people,[16] a people who shared a special covenant relationship with God, a people whom God referred to as his own son.[17] God desired for Israel to be a "flourishing olive tree, beautiful with well-formed fruit."[18]

This is our spiritual heritage as followers of Christ, and when we realize the truth of this grafting process in our own lives, its full meaning has the power to change everything for our future.

Our Spiritual Heritage

Imagine if we put as much energy into discovering our spiritual heritage—what we have inherited in Christ and what promises God has made to us—as we sometimes do when we attempt to find out about our natural heritage.

For example, a few years ago my sister-in-law caught the genealogy bug like millions of people around the world, and she went on a quest to find out as much as she could about her and Nick's family ancestry. Nick is the twelfth of thirteen children, and she spent an entire year following up on contacts and connections while building a solid family tree that went back generations. When she shared all her research with us, our daughters, Catherine and Sophia, loved reading through their family history about the interesting and somewhat colorful people who were part of Nick's family tree.

My family tree, however, is not quite so interesting. It looks more like a stick with one small branch, even though I have loads of relatives. This is because when I was thirty-three, I found out I was adopted. After doing a little digging, the only information I could find was the name of my biological mother. Consequently, I have so many questions about my ancestry, but whenever I try to fill in the gaps, I keep hitting a wall. Someday I will probably pursue other options to find out more details about my biological background, because my girls really want to know more about my side of the family.

I imagine there's something inside us all that wants to know where we came from and how that shaped who we are, but the truth is, our natural family history can only tell us so much. It's our spiritual heritage in God that tells us who we truly are and what we have in Christ. "In the first chapter of Ephesians, the apostle Paul lists the spiritual blessings of our inheritance."[19]

"He chose us in him . . . to be holy and blameless in love
    before him" (v. 4).
"He predestined us to be adopted" (v. 5).

"His glorious grace [was] lavished on us" (v. 6).

"We have redemption through his blood" (v. 7).

"We have . . . forgiveness of our trespasses" (v. 7).

"You also were sealed with the promised Holy Spirit . . . the down payment of our inheritance" (vv. 13–14).[20]

This list doesn't even scratch the surface of all that we have in Christ, but it's a start. Because of that, if we got more enthusiastic about digging into our spiritual ancestry, much like Nick's sister did for their family history, then I'm convinced it would change our everyday life. I know that what has held me strong in times of challenges, trials, suffering, betrayals, failures, heartaches, and attacks on my confidence is knowing whose I am and who I am—something I can find only in Jesus and God's Word.

We Are Fully Accepted

When Nick and I first welcomed Catherine into our lives, we immediately accepted her fully and completely into our family. We felt the same when Sophia was born. Initially, all they both did was cry, poo, eat, and sleep—still we accepted them just as they were. They didn't have teeth; they couldn't walk; they couldn't do anything for themselves. But the truth is they didn't have to do anything to impress Nick or me, much less achieve anything extraordinary. They were our children, and we loved them unconditionally. They had access to everything we had, especially our hearts. To say we were over the moon doesn't even come close to how much we adored them—and still do.

That's how God loves us but even better because, unlike

Nick and I who are imperfect parents for sure, God is a perfect father.[21] There is nothing in him but good.[22] And the moment we completely surrender ourselves to Jesus, this is the love and acceptance we encounter. We are grafted into the family of God, and there's nothing we can do to get grafted out. Paul wrote, "He predestined us to be adopted as sons through Jesus Christ for himself, according to the good pleasure of his will, to the praise of his glorious grace that he lavished on us in the Beloved One."[23]

We are 100 percent, fully accepted in the Beloved—in God's beloved Son with whom God said he was well pleased.[24] "To accept means to receive willingly, to regard with approval, to value, to esteem, to take pleasure in or to receive with favor . . . the Father has accepted us willingly, with approval, with value, with esteem, with delight, not because we have in any way merited his approval, but because his Beloved paid the price in full for our approval."[25]

Let that sink in. When Jesus was on the cross, he was forsaken by his Father that we might be accepted.[26] He took all the rejection, including self-rejection, we could ever face. Therefore, we are not accepted because of our behavior but because of our Savior. We are loved unconditionally not because of our behavior but because of our Savior. We are seen and known and chosen not because of our behavior but because of our Savior.[27] What's more, Jesus is the object of the Father's unconditional love and devotion. Because we are in Christ, we are also the objects of the Father's unconditional love and devotion—and nothing can separate us from his love.

This is exactly what Paul wrote to the church in Rome: "For I am persuaded that neither death nor life, nor angels nor rulers, nor things present nor things to come, nor powers, nor height nor depth, nor any other created thing will be able to separate us from the love of God that is in Christ Jesus our Lord."[28]

God wants us to truly have this understanding. Another reminder that we are his chosen ones, holy and beloved, is found in Colossians 3:12. In this verse, the word translated as "beloved" or "dearly loved" comes from the Greek word *agapaó*, which comes from *agape*, meaning "love." The tense used here is significant because it means that God has loved us in the past, he still loves us in the present, and he will continue to love us in the future.[29] Clearly, nothing can separate us from the love of God that is in Jesus, not even time.

How important then that we keep our eyes on Jesus, the one who loves us unconditionally and eternally, the one who accepts us no matter what we've done or what's been done to us. But when we take our eyes off Jesus and stop looking to him for our identity, value, worth, and acceptance, we naturally start looking for those things in other places or people. We start looking to our education, achievements, and socioeconomic status. We start looking to our spouses, children, and families. We start looking to our friendships and networks. We start looking at how many are following us on social media or like and share our posts. We place our value, identity, worth, significance, and security in the hands of other people, taking them away from our heavenly Father. And when we do, we lose sight of who we really are and how much we are truly loved and accepted in the Beloved.

I don't know what kind of home you grew up in, and I'm fully aware that while we all come from imperfect homes, some of us come from ones that were painfully abusive and damaging. I know I did, though my parents—who loved me dearly—had no idea what was happening to me during my growing-up years.

Whatever homelife you had, let me give us all a loving reminder: Even if your family of origin was deeply wounding and didn't give you a great start in life; even if you didn't have a great family tree full of loving branches who could help you grow and thrive; even if your family loved Christ but still didn't get it quite right; if you are in Christ today, your history does not have to define your destiny.

Your identity is in Christ—not in where you came from, not in what's been said to you, and not even in what's been done to you. You were created in the image of God on purpose for a purpose, and God is for you, wanting to help you fulfill all his plans and purpose for you.[30] Because you are an heir to the promises of God, you have a future, and according to Jeremiah 29:11, it's a future filled with hope. You are a child of God, a son or daughter of the King of kings—and nothing can change that. "And I will be a Father to you, and you will be sons and daughters to me, says the Lord Almighty."[31]

Even if your parents didn't want you and you were labeled a mistake, illegitimate, or accidental, you are now part of a royal family—the family of God—and you are wanted. And you're certainly not a mistake. "You are a chosen race, a royal priesthood, a holy nation, a people for his possession, so that you may proclaim the praises of the one who called you out of darkness into his marvelous light."[32]

Since it's obvious that we need to be rooted and grounded in Christ to live flourishing and fruitful lives, how do we do that? It's a great and important question. There is no one way, but there are things I've discovered throughout my journey following Jesus that have proven effective for me. I've developed spiritual practices that keep me connected to Jesus, strengthen my intimacy with him, and keep me rooted in him. These practices aren't new—they're spiritual disciplines that have been practiced by followers of Jesus throughout the history of the church. In one generation such practices were referred to as "practicing the presence of God." For another, it was called "communion with God." For another, it was known as "setting your mind." When Jesus walked the earth, he called it "abiding."

> Abide in Me, and I in you. As the branch cannot bear fruit of itself, unless it abides in the vine, neither can you, unless you abide in Me. I am the vine, you are the branches. He who abides in Me, and I in him, bears much fruit; for without Me you can do nothing. If anyone does not abide in Me, he is cast out as a branch and is withered; and they gather them and throw them into the fire, and they are burned. If you abide in Me, and My words abide in you, you will ask what you desire, and it shall be done for you.[33]

When we abide in Jesus—when we develop spiritual practices in our own lives—we are feeding our spiritual selves and nourishing our roots so that they run deep. In fact, we could say that spiritual practices are to our roots what fertilizer is to plants and trees. *Fertilizer* is the term for a "natural or artificial substance containing the chemical elements that improve growth and productiveness of plants. Fertilizers enhance the natural fertility of the soil or replace chemical elements taken from the soil by previous crops."[34] When we engage in spiritual practices or disciplines that enhance the fertility of our heart's soil, it becomes a place where seeds can grow into flourishing plants—like an olive tree planted in the house of God.[35]

The spiritual practices we can incorporate into our lives include the many ways that God's Word says we encounter him—reading the Bible, engaging in prayer, practicing silence and solitude, engaging in worship, being part of a local church community, taking a Sabbath rest, fasting, serving, and being generous with our resources.

One of the most effective ways for us to root ourselves in Christ is to immerse ourselves in all that God says about us—and to allow his Holy Spirit to penetrate our lives with his truth. It's how we renew our minds according to his Word.[36] As you read the following verses, let God's Word begin telling you who you are, and let it root you more deeply in his love.

You are loved.

- And we have come to know and to believe *the love that God has for us*. God is love, and the one who remains in love remains in God, and God remains in him. (1 John 4:16)
  - We love because *he first loved us*. (1 John 4:19)

You are seen.

- I will instruct you and show you the way to go; *with my eye on you*, I will give counsel. (Psalm 32:8)
  - *The eyes of the LORD are on the righteous*, and his ears are open to their cry for help. (Psalm 34:15)
  - As for you, LORD, you know me; *you see me*. (Jeremiah 12:3)

You are known.

- *Lord, you have searched me and known me.* You know when I sit down and when I stand up; you understand my thoughts from far away. You observe my travels and my rest; you are aware of all my ways. Before a word is on my tongue, you know all about it, Lord. You have encircled me; you have placed your hand on me. (Psalm 139:1–5)
- My sheep hear my voice, *I know them*, and they follow me. (John 10:27)

You are chosen.

- *I chose you* before I formed you in the womb; I set you apart before you were born. (Jeremiah 1:5)
- You did not choose me, but *I chose you.* I appointed you to go and produce fruit and that your fruit should remain, so that whatever you ask the Father in my name, he will give you. (John 15:16)

You are fully accepted.

- Therefore, accept each other just as Christ has *accepted you* so that God will be given glory. (Romans 15:7 NLT)
- Then Peter replied, "I see very clearly that God shows no favoritism. In every nation *he accepts those who fear him and do what is right.*" (Acts 10:34–35 NLT)

Because of all this, you can live like an olive tree, thriving and flourishing, in every season of life. You can say of your life

what David said when he was running for his life, being persecuted and threatened, and hiding from his enemies: "But I am
like a flourishing olive tree in the house of God; I trust in God's
faithful love forever and ever."[37]

That is the beauty of being rooted in Christ, of being grafted
into the family of God, of being loved by him, of abiding in him
and growing deeper roots throughout our lives.

LESSONS LEARNED

- When we have strong spiritual roots that go deep in God, we can live a life of faith, endurance, perseverance, and resilience, moving forward through whatever life throws our way and still fulfilling all the plans and purposes God has for us.
- Because we have been grafted into the family of God, we are accepted fully and unconditionally.
- God's love for us is past, present, and future. There's nothing we can do to be separated from his love.

QUESTIONS FOR REFLECTION

- Can you identify ways you currently fertilize your roots so they grow deep?
- Can you identify new ways you want to fertilize your roots so you bear good fruit?
- Can you feel that God loves, sees, knows, and accepts you fully as his beloved?
- If you don't feel God's love, what verses can you begin meditating on to renew your heart and mind to his truth?

Lesson 2

Behold the Beauty of God

Closing my eyes and taking a deep breath, I did my best to inhale as much of the sweet smell of the olive tree blossoms as I could. With their licorice-like floral scent, they saturated the countryside with a flurry of white flowers. Nick and I were in Spain with our girls and had taken a day trip to the countryside so I could see the trees in bloom—and we had come at just the right time.

When I stepped out of the car and began walking under the trees, the fragrance was so strong, it was all I could smell. Bending a branch down so I could see a bloom up close, I was fascinated that each flower was tiny, no bigger than my thumbnail, and showcased four petals with a yellowish-orangey center. They grew in clusters along the branches, changing the picturesque trees from silvery green to snowy white.

When I asked the farmer who managed the grove if all olive trees made such beautiful flowers, he said yes but also told me that there are as many as five hundred cultivars of olive trees and not all flowers look the same—though the hope is that every flower will produce an olive. Being the inquisitive type and thinking of all the kinds of flowers that five hundred types of trees could produce, I wondered: *When David wrote, "I am like a flourishing olive tree in the house of God,"[1] how did he know which type of olive tree to be like?* God didn't specify for David or any of us to be an Arbequina, Coratina, or a Picholine. He didn't say to be a Kalamata, Manzanilla, or Amfissa. He didn't say to be a Sevillano, Mission, or Nicoise. He just said for us to be like an olive tree, so I suppose it doesn't really matter. But what he did make clear that does matter is what Hosea wrote: Our "beauty shall be like the olive tree," and our "fragrance like [the cedars and aromatic shrubs of] Lebanon."[2]

As I lingered there, utterly overcome by the beauty of God—who created the beauty right in front of me—my heart, my mind, and my mouth began overflowing with fresh praise. Standing in a sea of blooms, beholding what looked like little stars twinkling in the breeze, I understood Hosea's words like never before. I found myself praying that, as I was rooted in Jesus and abiding in him, I would reflect the beauty of God as fragrantly, faithfully, and visibly as the trees that surrounded me.

That day I didn't leave as the same person I'd been when I arrived, because that's what beholding the beauty of God does. It changes and transforms us as it captivates us. That's why I enjoy nothing more than getting outdoors and seeing the beauty God has surrounded us with. Whether it's hiking a mountain, running on a beach, or riding my bike along a neighborhood path, I can never get enough of seeing what only God could have made.

Not long ago I had the opportunity to hike in the Patagonia region of Argentina, and I could barely take it all in. I trekked the Cerre Llao Llao trail in Bariloche, where there were snow-capped peaks in the distance, rocky ones in the foreground, and the most luscious green cypress and beech trees along the trail. I even got to see a type of myrtle tree that has cinnamon-colored bark. And the lakes scattered between the mountains were the most beautiful blue, crystal clear and cold. When I made my way to the shoreline of one lake, I could see through the water to all the pebbles resting on the bottom. They were smooth and in shades of colors only God could have designed. My senses were on serious overload, so much so that I almost cried. I don't know how God's beauty moves you or if you get outdoors enough to enjoy his magnificent displays, but I find God's beauty endless because it's reflected in *all* his creation.[3]

Seeing and experiencing God's beauty has the power to give us life in so many ways. Whether we're taking in a field of wildflowers, the sunlight glistening on a lake, or the green space of a park, all of these environments can affect us—mentally, emotionally, and physically. They even have the power to reduce our stress, to lower our blood pressure and our heart rate, all by bringing us a sense of calm. Study after study shows that spending time outdoors can help us focus on more positive emotions, improve our memory, and increase our ability to multitask. Such experiences can even improve our sleep and increase our levels of vitamin D, an essential nutrient for our health and well-being.[4]

Knowing all this, it's no wonder people are so captivated by God's beauty in creation. It has so many benefits! But while such physiological benefits are good, they are not creation's primary purpose. God's beauty on display in nature is a sign that points beyond itself, because it captivates our attention and directs our gaze from the creation to the Creator. In Psalm 19:1 we read, "The heavens declare the glory of God, and the expanse proclaims the work of his hands." And we are told in the book of

Romans, "For his invisible attributes, that is, his eternal power and divine nature, have been clearly seen since the creation of the world, being understood through what he has made."[5]

> God's beauty on display in nature is a sign that points beyond itself, because it captivates our attention and directs our gaze from the creation to the Creator.

If you've ever stood on the beach and watched the waves crash powerfully onto the shore, or marveled at the vastness of a mountain range and wondered about the one who is infinitely greater—the one who created all that you're seeing—then you know the captivating nature of the beauty of God. It draws our attention so that we will look to him. And when we do, we find one who is like no other. One who captivates our attention to capture our hearts.

Turn Your Gaze Toward God

As much as I love gazing at the beauty of God's creation, I have to admit that there is nothing more beautiful than gazing at the beauty of the actual Creator himself. David expressed this sentiment when he wrote, "I have asked one thing from the LORD; it is what I desire: to dwell in the house of the LORD all the days of my life, gazing on the beauty of the LORD and seeking him in his temple."[6]

When David penned those words, he was fleeing from his

son Absalom, who was conspiring to take his throne. In the midst of the chaos, David took time to gaze upon the beauty of God. The word *gaze* comes from the Hebrew word *chazah*, which means "to see, perceive, to contemplate with pleasure; to look, to behold."[7] Therefore, gazing is not glancing. It's not casually looking. It's not stealing a glimpse. It's being fully focused on beholding the transcendent beauty of God. It's steadily and intently admiring God.[8] That's what David did.

Have you ever caught yourself gazing at something beautiful? Perhaps you love gazing at the stars or at a beautiful painting or an eagle soaring. I know it's no surprise, but for me it is likely to be the waves on an ocean, the view from a mountaintop, or a sunset.

Gazing at the beauty of creation or art is something we can readily understand because we can physically see those things with our natural eyes, but gazing upon the beauty of an invisible God can seem impossible to comprehend—precisely because we cannot see him. Of course, when Jesus walked on the earth, he was the image of the invisible God.[9] But even then Scripture makes clear that, physically speaking, he looked like a typical, ordinary person: "He didn't have an impressive form or majesty that we should look at him, no appearance that we should desire him."[10]

We live in a world where we tend to equate beauty with whatever we consider to be attractive physical features. We have been conditioned by culture and the media alike to look at people's external attributes to determine whether or not they are beautiful. There are entire industries that foster this perspective and, in the process, inadvertently skew ours. When we scroll through social media or peruse a fashion magazine, we can see that the world has clearly established who is deemed one of the "beautiful people" and who is not.

But when David gazed upon the beauty of God, he wasn't looking at any physical features because the Hebrew word used for *beauty* means "kindness, pleasantness or delightfulness."[11] True beauty really is below the surface, not observed with physical eyes but perceived with spiritual eyes or the eyes of the heart. The beauty of the Lord is seen in his attributes. In his holiness, majesty, and glory. In his sovereignty, power, and might.

When we take the time to turn our gaze toward God, to linger in our gazing, we see his beauty. And when we see his beauty, we are transformed.[12] When we remember how he has faithfully acted out of who he is in our lives—loving us, forgiving us, redeeming us, transforming us, and tending to our broken hearts. When we reflect on the times when he has graciously pulled us out of situations that we got ourselves into. When he has mercifully forgiven us for the same sin we committed yesterday and the day before and the day before that. When he has lovingly accepted us in the midst of others rejecting us. When we comprehend clearly how all the good that God has done for us—every single thing—has been an act of mercy and grace that is undue and undeserved, it changes us. And when we are transformed, then we can reflect God's beauty: his kindness, pleasantness, and delightfulness to our world.

Let People See the Gold in You

When I saw The Sacred Olive Tree high atop the Acropolis, the tree that started my obsession with all things olive tree, I couldn't help but notice that it was growing in dry, dusty, and barren soil. It wasn't blooming in a lush grove surrounded by hundreds of other trees, like the ones I saw in Spain. It was baking in the hot sun and surrounded by nothing but ancient ruins. And yet it was flourishing. It was blooming. Against all odds. And that spoke volumes.

Beauty in this world is found in what we can see—and it's found in what we can't see. Not all olive trees are growing in well-tended groves, clustered together, putting on a show of blossoms that are breathtaking to behold. Some are scattered throughout the world, standing alone in the ugliest of places, holding on in the harshest of climates, and still blooming every January through March, often when nothing else is. They're popping out blooms and radiating beauty right where they are planted. God's beauty. And there's no one there to see them. To smell them. To touch them. To post them on social media. But that doesn't make them less beautiful.

When we find ourselves in a dry and dusty place spiritually, when we're more aware of our own shortcomings, failures, trauma, pain, and brokenness than we are of the beauty of God, we can find it difficult to see ourselves as beautiful blossoms enhancing the world around us. And when we do gaze upon the beauty of the Lord, we may not be able to see ourselves reflecting his beauty at all. But the truth is, we don't have to wait until we're perfect and have everything under control to start gazing and start reflecting.

When we feel unworthy to gaze or it feels impossible to reflect, we need to remember that the cross is the gateway to having access to the beauty of God and being transformed by it.[13] We need to remember who we are as members of God's family—loved, seen, known, chosen, and fully accepted. We're people rooted in him, abiding in him. The redemptive work of Jesus restores all that's been marred by sin in our lives. Yes, we may carry scars and residue from our past, even though we have been forgiven and redeemed, but that doesn't mean we can't be used by God to be signposts of his beauty in this world, beauty that all originates in him.

> Remember that the cross is the gateway to having access to the beauty of God and being transformed by it.

And even if there is an area he is still healing, still restoring, still conforming, it doesn't negate all that he has already done! Think of what would have happened if the disciples had to wait to be used by Jesus until they perceived themselves as perfect—we all know they never could have been and we never can be on this side of eternity. The disciples would have missed all the moments and opportunities to be used as God's vessels, and we will, too, if we allow what is not yet to stop us from sharing what God has already accomplished and continues to accomplish in our lives. People don't need perfect. They need real. Real testimonies of real transformation that come from really beholding and really encountering and really being transformed by our real, risen Savior.

God knew what he was getting when he found, rescued, and redeemed us. He knows "we have this treasure in clay jars,"[14] and he has sent us into this fallen world to be his witnesses. It's not enough to enjoy the beauty of his creation that he gave us to behold. It's not enough to experience the beauty of our salvation and not share it. Even when we feel like fragments God is still lovingly mending back together, we're to bring into our world all that's beautiful, good, and true. To bring into our world all that's righteous, holy, and filled with his wonder. To bring into our world all that's compassionate, loving, and generous. To bring into our world a visible testimony of the matchless beauty of our God so they, too, can come to behold his beauty.

Go Make Something Beautiful

Just as there are five hundred varieties of olive trees, each with unique blooms, we are all created uniquely in the image of God to bring forth beauty so people can see the beauty of God—no matter where we're planted, no matter what our vocation or season of life. You may be a doctor, receptionist, chef, entrepreneur, inventor, sales associate, artist, journalist, architect, teacher, lawyer, activist, administrator, writer, accountant, barista, fashion designer, theologian, or cosmetologist; imagine if you saw your primary goal in all your endeavors as bringing forth beauty in the world around you. As helping people see the beauty of the Lord through the beauty of your life and work. When you treat a patient. When you serve a customer. When you prepare a beautiful meal. When you lead your team. When you train your children. When you volunteer in your community. When you care for your aging parents. When you stop and listen to someone's story. When you show up for your friends. When you pray a heartfelt prayer. When you weep with those who weep and rejoice with those who rejoice.[15] If we all started our day with this perspective, then imagine how different our world would be.

I always tell our A21 team that it's about the one. If we can reach one person and educate them about the dangers of human trafficking. If we can rescue one person from the horror of human trafficking. If we can restore one person through our aftercare program, then we are taking the beauty of God to our world. One person at a time. We're helping people see something that is utterly inexhaustible—the beauty of God.

Our youngest, Sophia, is attending a university in Paris, where she's studying creative writing, comparative literature, and screenwriting. We've been on this journey of discovery since her middle school years, watching her go from reciting every line of *Hamilton* and wanting to be an actor in films and on Broadway to being a comedian—and I love that she's decided to pursue this dream God has put in her heart.

I can only imagine how her creativity will be stirred as she is immersed in the beauty of Paris—a city dating back to the third century that's known for its breathtaking sights: the iconic Eiffel Tower, the twelfth-century Notre Dame, the Louvre Museum, the ornate bridges, architecture, fashion houses, and sidewalk cafes. Its patisseries filled with baguettes, croissants, pains au chocolat, madeleines, and macarons. No doubt I've made you hungry, and I apologize if you have to run and grab a pastry, but the beauty of Paris is so vast, I suspect that even after four years of school, Sophia won't have seen it all.

So much more is the beauty of God. Even if we gaze at his beauty for a lifetime, we'll never exhaust all there is to see. We'll never exhaust becoming what we behold. We'll never exhaust the ways we can abide in him and reflect his beauty to our world. His kindness. His pleasantness. His delightfulness. And all the rest that he is. That is what we glean from the beautiful flowers of the olive tree.

LESSONS LEARNED

- Seeing and experiencing God's beauty has the power to give us life and lasting fruitfulness in so many ways.
- God's beauty on display in nature is a sign that points beyond itself, because it captivates our attention and directs our gaze from the creation to the Creator.
- Gazing is not glancing. It's being fully focused on beholding the transcendent beauty of God.

QUESTIONS FOR REFLECTION

- Hosea wrote: Our "beauty shall be like the olive tree," and our "fragrance like [the cedars and aromatic shrubs of] Lebanon."[16] How might that be in your life?
- How has seeing God's beauty transformed you?
- How do you see the beauty of God in others?

Lesson 3

Nourish Your Heart

Carrying a lawn chair out to our front yard, I picked a spot to sit where I could feel the warmth of the sun but have a bit of shade. I'd been inside all day and just needed a breath of fresh air. Before I could get settled and lost in my thoughts, I began to think of how the olive trees in our yard not only provide shade for me but are a safe haven for birds, squirrels, and who knows how many insects and bacteria and microorganisms that I know nothing about. To my naked eye, they are beautiful trees I can never get enough of, but to migrating birds and squirrels and other critters too small for me to see, they are a world of biodiversity.

All around the world, olive groves and their surrounding environments foster an ecosystem where a number of species coexist. Studies have determined that olive farms can support up to 200 wild plant species, 90 vertebrate species, and 160 invertebrate species for every two and a half acres.[1] Can you imagine? Many animals also depend on olive groves: From quail to partridges to sparrows to hoopoe, birds build their nests in and take food from the trees for their survival. Squirrels and lizards are equally at home, as are raccoons, who thoroughly enjoy eating olives.[2] While we may look at a grove of olive trees and see only trees and olives, an entire community is being supported and sheltered whose life and sustenance is facilitated by the grove. It's as though the olive grove is the heartbeat of an entire ecosystem—and it is.

I know you don't want a science lesson, so let me just say that in the same way God created an olive grove to be the heartbeat of an entire ecosystem, he created us with a heart at the very center of our spiritual well-being. And the condition of our heart affects every aspect of our lives.

Proverbs 4:23 tells us to "guard your heart above all else, for it is the source of life." This tells me that if I want to live a life that's flourishing like an olive tree, then the condition of my heart has to be flourishing too—because my spiritual heart is the source of my spiritual health. It's the seat of my emotions, the place from where I make decisions, the barometer, if you will, for how I'm doing overall. And it's this for you too. We need to give our spiritual hearts the same kind of attention and care that we give our physical hearts. And our spiritual hearts need a checkup just as much as our physical hearts do.

> If I want to live a life that's flourishing like an olive tree, then the condition of my heart has to be flourishing too—because my spiritual heart is the source of my spiritual health.

Despite how we may often separate our hearts from our intellect as two distinct things, the Bible does not; rather it combines the elements of mind, will, and emotions together with language about an organ (heart) that can feel, think, and act.[3] The way we think, talk, and act flows from our hearts.[4] Our character is formed from our hearts.[5] "For as [a person] thinks in his heart, so is he."[6]

It's in our spiritual hearts that we decide to follow Jesus and begin to love him with all our heart, soul, mind, and strength.[7] "If you confess with your mouth, 'Jesus is Lord,' and believe in your heart that God raised him from the dead, you will be saved. One believes with the heart, resulting in righteousness, and one confesses with the mouth, resulting in salvation."[8]

Conversely, it's equally true that from our hearts come everything we don't want in our lives: "For from within, out of people's hearts, come evil thoughts, sexual immoralities, thefts, murders, adulteries, greed, evil actions, deceit, self-indulgence, envy, slander, pride, and foolishness. All these evil things come from within and defile a person."[9]

I can't remember a time when what I was thinking in my head and acting out in my life wasn't affected by the condition of my heart. How important then for us to grow in our under-standing about our hearts so we keep flourishing—like an olive tree whose leaves are healthy and green, that's bursting with the beauty of flowers, that's popping out olive after olive.

All Roads Lead to Our Hearts

There's no doubt that over the past few years, our minds and hearts have felt like they've been on a roller-coaster ride of highs and lows, of wins and losses, of gratitude and utter disappointment.

We have lived through a global pandemic. There have been major political, economic, and environmental upheavals that have disrupted our world, and the outbreak of more wars and conflicts has only added to it. Then, when we consider what we might be experiencing personally in our families, in our friendships, in our work, in our churches and communities—well, the stress and anxiety of it all can take a toll.

With all this in mind, I can understand why the number of people seeking mental health treatment is almost twice as high as it was two decades ago.[10] Of course, I understand people are probably more comfortable with the idea of seeking help than ever before, and that is probably reflected in this increase. But it also clearly reflects that our hearts are overrun and in need of attention.

If you've read any of my previous books, you will know that for me, all roads lead back to the condition of our hearts. I have shared my own journey of childhood trauma, and I know every one of us has experienced differing levels of pain, suffering, loss, grief, betrayal, rejection, hurt, discouragement, failure, or disappointment in some form. None of us are without scars, and most of us have become weary simply living in this fallen world. For this reason we must determine to do as the scripture says: to guard our hearts.[11]

Three of the four Gospels record that Jesus devoted an entire parable to the understanding that having a healthy heart leads to spiritual growth—and having an unhealthy heart hinders our spiritual growth. He said when the Word we hear falls on the good ground of our hearts, it flourishes and bears fruit. But when it falls on ground unfavorable for growth, we perish. Sitting by the sea, he told a crowd of people:

Consider the sower who went out to sow. As he sowed, some seed fell along the path, and the birds came and devoured them. Other seed fell on rocky ground where it didn't have much soil, and it grew up quickly since the soil wasn't deep. But when the sun came up, it was scorched, and since it had no root, it withered away. Other seed fell among thorns, and the thorns came up and choked it. Still other seed fell on good ground and produced fruit: some a hundred, some sixty, and some thirty times what was sown. Let anyone who has ears listen.[12]

Jesus used this analogy to show us that our hearts are where the seed of the Word of God falls and flourishes—if the soil of our hearts is receptive. But as the story shows us, there are four possible conditions we can have: a hard heart, a shallow heart, a crowded heart, or a fruitful heart. It's totally up to us.

Jesus wants our hearts to be good soil. If we learn to cultivate the soil of our hearts well, to guard them above all else from callousness, apathy, unrepentance, offense, bitterness, anger, resentment, unforgiveness, and anything else that can make it hard, shallow, or crowded, then we can continue to grow in our faith.

So often, in order to initiate change in our lives, we reach for all the external things we can adjust, but what this verse makes clear is that it's the condition of our hearts *internally* that determines the course of our lives *externally*—because everything in our lives flows from our hearts.

> It's the condition of our hearts *internally* that determines the course of our lives *externally*—because everything in our lives flows from our hearts.

Therefore, it is imperative that we learn how to protect the spiritual organ that keeps us alive and thriving—so we don't wind up wounded and hurting, sick and tired, toxic and bitter, having a spiritual heart attack and in need of a spiritual hospital.

Because I understand that my physical heart will one day give out and I will die, I do all I can to extend its life. I eat as healthy as I can, avoiding too many fatty foods, carbs, and sugary treats. I exercise daily. And I get those preventative annual checkups to ensure that the work I'm putting into my body is effective and that there's not something more I need to be doing. In other words, I take care of my physical heart. I protect it. I nourish it. I pay attention to what I'm putting into my body so I'll be able to run my race and finish my course.

In similar fashion, because I don't want to die spiritually at any point, I guard the condition of my spiritual heart. To *guard* anything is the act of protecting or defending it, whatever it is.[13] When we think of this in the context of the military, for example, we think of soldiers standing guard, ready to defend who and what they're protecting. The times I've been in London and walked past Buckingham Palace and seen The King's Guard, I have understood that if anyone behaves in a threatening way, the Guard will take action. They look quite ornamental with their red uniforms and tall fur hats, but in reality they are fully trained and operational military personnel.[14] What The King's Guard does most of the time, however, is *stand guard*.

To stand guard is "to keep watch in order to look for possible danger or threats."[15] The ESV translation of Proverbs 4:23 uses the phrase "keep your heart with all vigilance." *To keep our hearts* can be expressed as to "watch your mind" or "keep a hand on your head."[16] I especially like that last definition because I often literally place my hand on my forehead and speak Scripture over myself. It's one of the ways I guard my thoughts and keep them on track and in alignment with God and his thoughts, particularly when they want to spiral.

We live in an age when it's so easy to be bombarded by more opinions than we can process. One five-minute scroll of social media and we'll have a week's worth of advice, ideas, and thoughts to process—and much of it negative or disheartening. It's so easy for our minds to be overloaded and left unguarded.

One thing I hear a lot these days is well-meaning people telling us to follow our hearts, or to listen to our hearts. Yet the Bible says, "The heart is deceitful above all things, and desperately sick; who can understand it?"[17] I'm writing this in an airport, and only minutes before—while walking through a bookstore to grab a coffee—I saw four book titles that all had to do with listening to your heart, following your heart, or chasing your heart.

I don't know the full content of any of those books, but the titles are all bad advice, because God wants us to go to him in regard to our hearts. He wants us to follow after him and seek him first.[18] He wants us to have a heart after his heart, like David did.[19] And to do this well, we have to guard the condition of our hearts.

If you've never heard someone tell you that you have the ability to control your mind, to control your thoughts, and to choose what you think on night and day, I want to remind you that you absolutely can control your thoughts. In Colossians 3:2 Paul exhorted us to set our minds on things above, and in Philippians 4:8 he gave us a list of things we are to dwell on, including "whatever is true, whatever is honorable, whatever is just, whatever is pure, whatever is lovely, whatever is commendable—if there is any moral excellence and if there is anything praiseworthy—dwell on these things." We have the ability through the power of the Holy Spirit to consciously set our minds on the things we choose to dwell on. We don't have to be subject to every thought thrown our way. Jesus has given us great power over our own minds—and the power to guard our hearts.

But What About When . . . ?

But what about when we have made every effort to guard the condition of our hearts but something that is not good has found its way in? What about when our hearts are sick, even severely sick? Is there hope then?

The beautiful mystery of abiding in Christ is that if we inadvertently stop producing good fruit, he will always be faithful to show us areas in our lives where we're not abiding. That's right—it's entirely possible that as we abide in Christ, we will discover places in our hearts that are hindering our intimacy with him and our capacity to receive his love. And those are the places where something has taken root and needs to be uprooted.

To uproot is "to pull up by the roots; to remove as if by pulling up."[20] Sometimes the things that need uprooting in our hearts are a result of painful experiences we've had, or how we were raised, or what was said to us, or even because of the deceptive nature of our own hearts. It's in those areas of our hearts that we've been wounded and need to experience the healing that only Jesus can give. Jesus said that "My Father is glorified by this: that you produce much fruit and prove to be my disciples."[21]

Therefore, anything that causes us to be fruitless or to bear bad fruit needs to be uprooted.

There are many things that can compromise the condition of our hearts and cause us to need healing and become unfruitful or bear bad fruit. This is why we must pay attention to the kind of nutrients we are pouring into the soil of our hearts, and whether they are nutritious for bearing much fruit for the glory of God—or proving to be toxic for our spiritual growth and maturity.

The things that can be toxic can include the friendship circles we have, what we watch and listen to, what we think about, the social media accounts we follow, what we talk about, the habits we develop, and myriad other things. It's so important that we take a regular inventory of what we allow to take root in our hearts and how we are nourishing these roots so that we can uproot what's causing us to be unfruitful or to be producing bad fruit. In the words of the prophet Jeremiah, there are times in life "to uproot and tear down, to destroy and overthrow, to build and to plant."[22]

I know in my early years as a Christ follower, I found deep roots in my heart that had to be pulled up. For example, dealing with hurt, rejection, and offense was difficult for me, mostly because of the trauma I had endured in my formative years. I was a follower of Jesus but my heart was full of unforgiveness, bitterness, hurt, offense, rejection, and anger because of the abuse, abandonment, and rejection that shaped me. But the deeper I grew in Christ—by abiding in the Word of God, by spending time worshiping and being with Jesus—the more I was able to work on renewing my mind, the more healing I experienced in my heart, and the more I matured and transformed. Nothing can change us like being in the presence of God himself. In time, as I grew more resilient, loving, and forgiving, I found that I could live free from the offense, anger, unforgiveness, and bitterness that at first had been so hard to overcome. The soil of my heart had changed—as did the condition of my heart—because I had been starving the toxic emotions that had taken root and had begun feeding my heart with healthy nutrients from the Word of God. The strongest way to move our hearts from bearing bad fruit to producing good fruit will always be abiding in Jesus.

The First Step to Healing

As we have seen in our study, David—the same David who testified, "But I am like a flourishing olive tree in the house of God; I trust in God's faithful love forever and ever"[23]—faced tremendous adversity. He was hated. He was hunted. He was persecuted. He suffered. He was dethroned. He was opposed. He was accused. He was abandoned. He was betrayed. And that's just the short list. And yet he was able to testify to the truth of God's love.

There can be countless things that break our hearts and, in some instances, make us feel like we will never recover. I have to believe David felt that way at times, and what we read elsewhere in the Psalms certainly seems to confirm it.

> Be gracious to me, LORD, for I am weak;
> heal me, LORD, for my bones are shaking;
> my whole being is shaken with terror.
> And you, LORD—how long? (6:2-3)
>
> I am weary from my groaning;
> with my tears I dampen my bed

and drench my couch every night.
My eyes are swollen from grief;
they grow old because of all my enemies. (6:6–7)

How long, LORD? Will you forget me forever?
How long will you hide your face from me?
How long will I store up anxious concerns within me,
agony in my mind every day?
How long will my enemy dominate me? (13:1–2)

My strength is dried up like baked clay;
my tongue sticks to the roof of my mouth.
You put me into the dust of death. (22:15)

When olive trees are sick, it shows. You can see it—in the leaves, in the trunk, even in the fruitlessness. We are much the same way, and although what we're suffering from may not show immediately, eventually we will see it. And this is the first step to healing—recognizing that something is wrong.

Because everything flows from the heart, the fruit of our lives—the way we live, what we think, what we say, what we do, what we give our time and money to, and so much more—can tell us about the state of our hearts. And when what is being produced isn't good—whether it's apathy, anger, bitterness, hopelessness, unforgiveness, wastefulness, purposelessness, fear, vindictiveness, entitlement, selfishness, greed, or something else—it tells us that something is wrong. Not just with the situation, the circumstance, the decision, or someone else's actions—although any of those may be a factor—but within us and our hearts.

Recognize that this is where our heart healing begins, but it's not where it ends. When horticulturalists identify a sick olive tree, they don't focus just on the signs of the sickness; they go after the source of the sickness[24]—whether it's too much sun, too little water, attacks from pests, or too little nutrition—and address it so that the tree can flourish again.

When we look at David, we see that he did the exact same thing. He addressed the source of sickness so that he could flourish again:

> When David's heart was sick with fear in Psalm 3, he recognized the source of the sickness—isolation. So he went to God, he got into the presence of God, and his heart was healed.
>
> When David's heart was sick with suffering and waiting in that suffering in Psalm 6, he recognized the source of the sickness—hopelessness, fear that there would be no end to it based on a lie. David reminded himself who God is—the God who hears and acts in justice—and his heart was healed.
>
> When David's heart was sick with being overwhelmed in Psalm 7, he recognized the source of the sickness—a loss of perspective and focus on God. What then resuscitated his heart? Lifting his eyes and worshiping God.
>
> When David's heart was sick with sin in Psalm 32, he recognized the source of his heart's sickness—unrepentance. He confessed and repented, and his heart was healed.
>
> When David's heart was sick with anxiety in Psalm 38, he recognized the source of his heart's sickness—sin. He confessed and repented, and his heart was healed.

When David's heart was sick with the weight of attack in Psalm 54, he recognized the source of his heart's sickness—that he was undefended. He recalled God's faithfulness and the past testimonies of deliverance, and his heart was healed.

Although I wish it wasn't the case, we will all find times when the symptoms, what's coming *out* of our hearts, show that what's *in* our hearts is not good. What do we do then? First, we don't conceal the symptoms. Then we get with God. We ask him to reveal the source: Is it too little nourishment or water from a lack of time in his Word or presence? Is it infection from sin we're harboring and unrepentance? Is it a lie or forgetfulness of the testimony? And we pray for God to show us and then we pursue what heals from that place.

I don't know the condition of your heart today, but I do know that it's never too late for God to heal your broken heart, mend your wounds, or revive your heart, even if it feels utterly dead.

> It's never too late for God to heal your broken heart, mend your wounds, or revive your heart, even if it feels utterly dead.

Even if . . .

People you thought you'd do life with forever have
   walked away.

A relationship you thought would go to the next level
    didn't.
A colleague that you helped to advance betrayed you.
You miscarried, again.
The adoption fell through.
You lost a job through no fault of your own.
You failed your college entrance exam.
Or you passed it, started school, but didn't get to finish.
You lost someone you loved all too soon.
One of your children strayed, and you're still waiting to see
    them restored.
You were passed over for a promotion.
You auditioned for a role, but you weren't chosen.
A deal for a new house fell through, just when you thought
    it was yours.
Your business failed after years of investing so much.
Your retirement funds and plans took a nose dive.
A diagnosis altered your life in ways you never saw
    coming.

And on I could go. I think we'd all agree that countless things can break our hearts and, in some instances, make us feel like we will never recover. But the Lord promises us that he "is near the brokenhearted; he saves those crushed in spirit."[25] He promises us that "he heals the brokenhearted and bandages their wounds."[26] And he keeps his promises.[27]

Because of that, we can love God with all our hearts, souls, and minds. We can accomplish all the plans and purpose he has for our lives. We can finish our race on this earth strong. I understand that requires us depending on the Holy Spirit to help us guard our hearts, to keep our hearts soft and tender, but whatever hurt comes our way, the truth is our hearts can be resuscitated. God can redeem every broken heart, every betrayed heart, every transgressed heart. God can heal us so we flourish again as an olive tree, and therein lies our hope.

LESSONS LEARNED

- Our spiritual hearts—revealed in our thoughts, words, and actions—determine our spiritual health.
- The condition of our hearts *internally* determines the course our lives will take *externally*.
- Because everything flows from the heart, the fruit of our lives—the way we live, what we think, what we say, what we do, what we give our time and money to, and so much more—can tell us about the state of our hearts.

QUESTIONS FOR REFLECTION

- How would you describe your spiritual health today?
- Is there something you're going through that makes you think you'll never recover?
- What steps can you take to improve your spiritual health and flourish again?

Lesson 4

Pursue Slow, Steady Growth

Patience is my least favorite word in the English language. If you were to ask anyone in my family or someone who works with me, most likely they would acknowledge that patience is not one of my strengths. I feel sure that somewhere in my spirit is this seed just waiting to sprout, but I know from the times when my patience has been tested that it has yet to come into full bloom.

It's not because I haven't fertilized it and watered it faithfully, because I have. For years. When I'm stuck in traffic. When I'm waiting because my flight has been delayed. Again. When I'm in the car, in the driveway, waiting on the girls to come get in the car. Still, patience remains a struggle. Even when I do something as basic as baking cookies, my lack of patience can get the best of me—and the cookies.

When my girls smell cookies baking, they come rushing to the kitchen, because they know I'm going to do one of two things. I'm either going to pull them out too soon, because I've got things to do and I can't stand waiting one more minute on them, or I'm going to wander off and start doing something else I need to do and completely forget about them. So I specialize in baking cookies that are either the equivalent of warm dough or quite well done—perhaps with some burned edges as a bonus. Suffice it to say, it's best that I leave the cookie baking to Catherine and Sophia. I have good intentions but not enough patience.

Still, I have used many a trying moment as an opportunity to change. I'm so grateful that God is patient, and that he is patient with me as I keep working on this. It's certainly not easy in a world where it feels like everything moves faster and faster every day—and for the most part, life at this speed works for us. It's convenient for sure, at least in most situations. We live in an instant gratification world where we can google anything and have answers in minutes. We can snap a picture and upload it to social media within seconds, with it instantly being available to everyone in the world who has access. We can order something online and have it delivered in the same day. But not everything in this life was meant to happen quickly. Some things were designed to take time . . . and for our good.

> Some things were designed to take time . . . and for our good.

I found this to be true more than ever in my study of the olive tree, because one of its distinct characteristics is that it grows at a snail's pace. It is not a fast-growing tree at all. If you plant a grove of olive trees, all in hopes of developing a profitable olive farm, then you better prepare yourself to wait a goodly number of years. In fact, it can take as many as ten years for an olive tree to begin producing its first olive. That's right, you most likely will have to wait roughly a decade before you can collect your first substantial harvest.[1] Now, if owning an olive tree farm is your dream, please don't let this discourage you, but don't wait either. Whatever your age, might I suggest that now would probably be a good time to get started, because it's going to take a while before you get to eat your first olive. And keep your day job, at least for the next ten years.

All jokes aside, from one year to the next before a tree ever produces the first olive, a lot of growth you can't see is happening—both underground and aboveground—and this is what makes the olive tree strong and sturdy. Years of slow, steady growth are what make the olive tree's wood some of the densest, most tightly grained in the world. The consistent slow pace of growing makes the wood not only hard but also dry, and therefore it's highly appreciated by woodcrafters. In fact, on the Janka hardness test, olive wood is harder than oak.[2]

It's no wonder that it has been used since ancient times to craft and build so many things. Its rich caramel color and straight grain, along with its fruity scent, has attracted artisans for centuries. Even as far back as when Solomon built the temple, he used cedar and cypress for the structure but olive wood for the inside. For the inner sanctuary he made two cherubim that were fifteen feet high with a wingspan of fifteen feet. For the entrance to that inner sanctuary, he made five-sided olive-wood doorposts and olive-wood doors on which he carved more cherubim, palm trees, and flower blossoms, which he then overlaid with gold.[3]

Today olive wood is still highly sought after, though it is not often harvested for lumber, as the trunks often grow twisted.[4] In my travels I've discovered that instead olive wood is used for everything from furniture to kitchen utensils to fruit bowls to chess sets to Nativity carvings.

Like an Olive Tree, Jesus Grew

Everything living in this world starts as a seed, including olive trees. Even we as people made in the image of God begin as a seed—and seeds take time to grow. None of us can fast-track our growth process—not physically or spiritually. And there's a reason for that: Slow, steady growth produces the character of Christ in us, and his character is the backbone of our purpose.

> Slow, steady growth produces the character of Christ in us, and his character is the backbone of our purpose.

To live a flourishing life and grow in Christ requires something from us. Our activity and God's actions are not independent. What we do matters. In Psalm 1, for example, we read about a tree that is planted by streams of water. It is flourishing and its leaves do not wither. What, if anything, contributed to that tree's flourishing? We aren't left guessing. In verses 1–2 we are told: "How happy is the one who does not walk in the advice of the wicked or stand in the pathway with sinners or sit in the company of mockers! Instead, his delight is in the LORD's instruction, and he meditates on it day and night."

This tree flourished as it turned *from* and turned *to*—it turned from sin and turned to God's Word. We are established in

Jesus, yes, but we have to keep growing in him and God's Word. Dr. Henry Cloud once said in reference to our spiritual growth, "You can't grow a plant by dipping it into the dirt once a year. It takes ongoing connection."[5]

Even when Jesus entered this world, he came as a newborn babe and had to grow like any other boy. I imagine Mary was as happy as I was that her firstborn didn't come into this world as a fully grown adult. Having given birth to two children, such an idea sounds not only preposterous but too hard for me to think about—even with an epidural.

Seriously, while we know that Jesus came into this world as a baby, what we don't know in any great detail is what his life was like on a daily basis *as he grew*. We don't know what his life was like as a toddler, as a little boy, as a preteen, then a teen, and as a young man. We do know he preached in the temple when he was twelve and started his earthly ministry at age thirty.[6] But what happened to him between the ages of twelve and thirty?

All the Bible tells us about those eighteen years is what Luke recorded in his first two chapters: "The boy grew up and became strong, filled with wisdom, and God's grace was on him."[7] "And Jesus increased in wisdom and stature, and in favor with God and with people."[8]

I love how Luke wrote that Jesus "grew up." That's what we're supposed to do in this life. It's simply not possible to leapfrog from spiritual infancy to spiritual adulthood. It's the course of a lifetime to grow into the image of Christ. In the Greek, the word *grew* comes from the same root word as *increase*. It is used to measure many things, including the maturation process.[9] The two verses just quoted from Luke 2 show us that Jesus matured. He increased. He grew internally while he was growing externally. Luke specifically says Jesus grew in wisdom, stature, and favor.

It would be so easy to glaze over how Jesus matured, but like the olive tree grows slowly and steadily, it's important that we learn the significance of these three words Luke used. Stick with me for a few paragraphs as we unpack these Greek words because they are full of insights. And besides that, why miss an opportunity to delve deeper into anything Greek? My mother would be so proud.

Wisdom: The Greek word for *wisdom* is *sophia.* It is accrued knowledge and the practical skills associated with living a successful life. These range from the ability to create highly skilled works to the intellectual capability required to make choices that result in favorable outcomes and avoid troubles.[10] It is also often associated with trust in and fear of God.[11]

Stature: This word, *hélikia*, refers to maturity, age, or lifespan.[12] It is also defined as the social recognition, qualifications, or expectations of a specific age group; behavior befitting an older age group often resulting in greater esteem in all categories of life.[13] It is also used to show the weakness of humanity and the need to rely on God as well as a way to measure the maturity of a Christian.[14]

Favor: *Favor* comes from the same word as *grace—charis.* It is defined as goodwill freely disseminated by God, especially to the benefit of the recipient regardless of the benefit accrued to the disseminator.[15] It represents God's graciousness and approval.[16]

Jesus grew—over time—in these ways. He grew in knowledge and the application of it, as well as in the practical skills needed for a successful life. He matured in his reliance on God as he matured physically. And he grew in God's grace; he grew in favor with God and people. If Jesus had to grow or mature in all these ways, then surely we do too. After all, our goal in this life is to become more like him—to become rooted, resilient, and fruitful—for his glory.[17]

Grow Where You Need to Go

Growing is a theme in the Bible. God watched his own Son grow and he loves to watch us grow. Growing is what we as Jesus followers are to do—we are to grow where we need to go, and slow, steady growth like the olive tree is what produces the character we need to get there. Remember, our character is the backbone to our purpose, so even when it's a bit painful, we have to be committed to growing slowly, consistently, and intentionally.

> Our character is the backbone to our purpose, so even when it's a bit painful, we have to be committed to growing slowly, consistently, and intentionally.

When Catherine, my eldest daughter, was a preteen and she would complain about her shins hurting or her hips aching, it was because she was growing. She was experiencing what we call growing pains. Sometimes I think we feel something similar in our spiritual walk. It often hurts to grow because growing involves stretching our spiritual muscles. It involves doing what we have never done before or going where we've never gone before. It involves trusting God when we'd rather avoid anything that feels like another risk—especially after we've been wounded, experienced trauma, or been rejected, disappointed, disillusioned, or blindsided by something that hurt us deeply. Still we are to grow.

Writing to the church in Ephesus, Paul said, "Let us grow in every way into him who is the head—Christ."[18] To his beloved church in Philippi, he wrote: "I pray this: that your love will keep on growing in knowledge and every kind of discernment."[19] To his protégé Timothy, he said, "Practice these things; be committed to them, so that your progress may be evident to all."[20]

Even Peter understood the need to grow, and of course after many immature slipups, he would have learned this the hard way. When he admonished the scattered, persecuted church, he said, "Like newborn infants, desire the pure milk of the word, so that by it you may grow up into your salvation."[21] He admonished us to "grow in the grace and knowledge of our Lord and Savior Jesus Christ."[22]

As Jesus followers, we're to have a posture of growth. *Posture* is a stance; it's "a conscious mental or outward behavioral attitude."[23] It's a poise we can carry.

When I see my girls with their shoulders slumped over, I'm quick to remind them to sit or stand up straight, to hold their shoulders back, to mind their posture. It's in those moments that I clearly hear myself sounding just like my mother talking to me when I was their age, and even though I find myself slumping over my computer from time to time, I want them to be mindful of how they are carrying themselves. I want them to have poise, to be conscious of their posture.

It's the same with our spiritual growth. We should maintain

a posture of growth throughout our lives—a conscious mental attitude that's intentional about it. Even though we will never arrive this side of eternity, we're always being conformed and transformed into the image of God. It would also be extremely arrogant if we felt we knew all about the Bible, God, Jesus, and the Holy Spirit and no longer needed to grow.

What's more, it's crucial that we recognize we have an active role in our own growth. At the same time, it's also important to know that God doesn't leave us on our own when it comes to our growth. In the same letters that Paul wrote telling us to keep growing, he also said, "For it is God who is working in you both to will and to work according to his good purpose."[24] He assured us that "he who has begun a good work in you will complete it until the day of Jesus Christ."[25] We are not in this on our own. He is always with us and helping us. I am so grateful for this because I know I couldn't do it on my own.

At the time of this writing, I am fifty-eight, and I assure you, I have not arrived. In fact, in many ways I feel as though I am just beginning. I believe that a major reason I am still so intrigued and enamored by Jesus is because I have maintained a posture of growth. Right this minute I'm sitting in the Athens airport waiting on my next flight, while planning further study options because I want to keep being effective and fruitful. I can keep bearing fruit only if I keep growing in Christ.

For example, Nick and I are in a season of watching our girls grow into adults. Sophia is in her first year of college and deciding what she wants to do with her future. Catie is about to graduate and is thinking of where life will take her next, something we discuss often. It would be weird if she still wanted to do the things she did as a toddler. I love that she spent one year studying in London, exploring more ideas for her future. Her desire to keep growing where she needs to is a sign of health.

God designed each and every one of us to grow—consistently, slowly, and at a steady pace. And despite the pressure we might feel in our fast-paced world filled with social media overnight-success stories and influencers with millions of followers, whose posts make anything and everything look easy, our spiritual growth will take patience and intentionality. It will take time, and I know from experience that it won't be easy, but it will always be worth it. God wants us to develop sustainable growth, the kind that builds strength and resilience in us in one season and prepares us for the next—the kind that supports us so we can fulfill all the purpose and plans he has in mind for us. The kind that makes us grow up to be like an olive tree—strong and sturdy.

LESSONS LEARNED

- God wants us to grow strong and sturdy like the olive tree, but to do that we must grow slowly, consistently, and intentionally.
- Jesus's life models this for us. He grew up in wisdom, stature, and favor, meaning he showed us how to mature.
- When we start growing, we're not to stop. We're to keep maturing and becoming more like Christ as long as we live on this earth.

QUESTIONS FOR REFLECTION

- Can you identify ways you might try to rush your spiritual growth, perhaps because of being influenced by living in such a fast-paced world?
- Are there adjustments you can make to slow down and grow more intentionally?
- What spiritual practices can you add to your routines to stimulate future steady growth?

Lesson 5

Cultivate Humility

Being Greek, I am nothing if not passionate about, well, most everything. We Greeks are all in, meaning we talk loudly, we gesture with our hands, and we move our arms about wildly while doing so. We express every opinion with life-or-death conviction, whether we're right or wrong. At one point in my journey, I honestly tried to tone it down a bit, but after a while I realized it was no use, so I finally gave up on that. I am Greek and I will always be Greek—and that includes everything that comes with my Greekness. I also came to understand that passion can be a good thing, especially when it comes to following Jesus and remembering what he did for me.

People often ask me how I've maintained my passion for Jesus after all these decades. I truly think one of the main reasons is that I have never lost sight of the awe and wonder of being saved by the grace of God—and being made a part of the forever family of God. I think that if we truly understand what it cost God to graft us into the olive tree, to save us, to atone for our sins, and to make us a part of his family, then there can be no other response but one of humility and gratitude. We did not earn this and we do not deserve this. Yet God, out of his great love for us, his great grace, and his faithfulness to his promises, chose to save us and graft us wild olive shoots into the cultivated olive tree.

I remember what I was like before Jesus saved me. I remember the shame, the guilt, the condemnation, the helplessness, and the hopelessness I carried. I remember what it was like to be lost and then found, to have been spiritually blind and then able to see. I remember what I felt when I realized that Jesus died for me while I was yet a sinner, that I did not have to clean myself up to come to him, and that he came for me in my brokenness and pain. Jesus not only forgave me of my sins, which was more than I deserved, but also gave me a brand-new life here on earth, made me a part of a brand-new family, and gave me a purpose and hope for the future. What kind of God would do that? Only Jesus.

And yet, I'll admit, in my humanity there have been times when I've forgotten. When humility has escaped me and pride has crept in. It's something I realize we all wrestle with from time to time. Even when Paul wrote to the early Christians about being grafted into the people of God, continuing to use the olive tree example, he went on to warn them about their attitude:

> Now if some of the branches were broken off, and you, though a wild olive branch, were grafted in among them and have come to share in the rich root of the cultivated olive tree, do not boast that you are better than those branches. But if you do boast—you do not sustain the root, but the root sustains you.[1]

To boast is "a statement expressing excessive pride in oneself, the act or an instance of boasting."[2] Ouch. None of us want to boast, do we? And yet we inadvertently do when we fail to walk in humility and ask God to search our hearts daily. After almost four decades of following Jesus, I have discovered that spiritual pride is a very dangerous thing because it always leads to thinking more highly of ourselves than we ought to and mistreating people. It's an example of what the Bible warns us against over and over when it says, "Be not wise in your own eyes,"[3] and it produces a vibe that says, "I am better than you; I am more holy than you; I am more worthy than you; I am more deserving than you." If we are not careful, feelings of superiority and self-righteousness can creep into our hearts, and there is nothing more unbiblical than thinking we are better than anyone else. And yet, because of our humanity, I imagine that we've all done it at one time or another.

Humility, on the other hand, is something else altogether. It's recognizing that "we are not self-sufficient, that we depend on God for all we need."[4] It's "the personal quality of being free from arrogance and pride and having an accurate estimate of one's worth."[5] It's the opposite of entitlement—"the belief that one is inherently deserving of privileges or special treatment."[6]

It's about having the right view of who God is—that he is God and we are not. It's about knowing who we are in Christ, believing that what God says is truer than what we think, and trusting that what God says about us is right. It's understanding that we don't have to be the biggest, the best, the richest, the smartest, or the fastest because our identity is in Christ and not in our performance or achievements. It's about knowing that what we are is a wild olive tree who's been grafted into the family of God, that we are people saved by grace who truly can do nothing apart from Jesus.[7]

The beauty of humility is that it helps us be free of concern for our own ego so that we can see others for who they are. It means that we don't have to spend our lives trying to prove ourselves. It also means that we don't have to spend our lives trying to protect ourselves, because we know that God has our back, and we are therefore free to elevate those around us. That means we're curious about others and we want God's best for them. We care about their well-being. We listen to them because we know that we don't know everything.

Humility is being teachable, approachable, authentic, grateful, forgiving, and gracious. It's seeking God for who he alone is and what he alone can provide while being fully reliant on and loyal to Jesus—all important and necessary qualities we need to keep growing in Christ. It's having an attitude of gratitude for "so great a salvation"[8]—an attitude that keeps our walk with Jesus fresh, dynamic, and more of a faith adventure than a boring religious obligation. It relieves us of the burden of having to be perfect, to be our own god, to feel the pressure to be in control, all-knowing, or all-powerful, which is impossible anyway.

With all this in mind, it's equally important to know that adopting an attitude of humility does not mean that we diminish ourselves, put ourselves down, minimize who God has created us to be, or think that we are less than who we are in Christ. That is not humility; that is living in denial of our God-given identity as sons and daughters of the King of kings. A. W. Tozer, who was an American pastor, author, and magazine editor, once said, "The victorious Christian neither exalts nor downgrades himself. His interests have shifted from self to Christ."[9]

Seek Humility

As powerful as humility is, it will never happen on its own; we have to cultivate it in our own lives and intentionally seek it as we grow in Christ. Zephaniah, one of the prophets in the Old Testament, wrote, "Seek the LORD, all you humble of the earth, who carry out what he commands. Seek righteousness, seek humility."[10]

When Paul wrote to the Colossians, he said that we're to clothe ourselves in humility.[11] We're to "put it on" just like we would a piece of clothing. Perhaps by wrapping ourselves in it, we won't lose the feeling of being ever so grateful for all that God has done for us and how far he's brought us, particularly when he uses us to further his kingdom purposes.

To truly understand how to work out humility in our lives, we need only look to Jesus. After all, even though he is God, he was also the most humble man who ever lived and walked the earth. Jesus is the ultimate example of what true humility looks like in the trenches of real life. In his letter to the Philippians, Paul said for us to have the same attitude as Jesus, which was an attitude of humility: "Do nothing out of selfish ambition or conceit, but in humility consider others as more important than yourselves. Everyone should look not to his own interests, but rather to the interests of others."[12] And then he went on to describe Jesus and how he lived this attitude of humility:

- "Existing in the form of God, [Jesus] did not consider equality with God as something to be exploited."
- Jesus "emptied himself by assuming the form of a servant, taking on the likeness of humanity."
- Jesus "humbled himself by becoming obedient to the point of death."[13]

Jesus was willing to lay down his rights and privileges to glorify God. He lived a life of service, obedience, and sacrifice. He modeled what it was to put others first and care for the poor, the marginalized, and the oppressed. He did not come to be served but to serve. As followers of Jesus we, too, should adopt the same attitude. In a world full of pride, arrogance, greed, narcissism, self-gratification, self-exaltation, selfies, platforms, marketing, and branding, it is not easy to adopt an attitude of humility. But if we want to be like Jesus, then we have to be willing to be humble on purpose.

The apostle James said we are to humble ourselves before the Lord, and that if we do, God will exalt us.[14] Peter wrote the same sentiment: "Humble yourselves, therefore, under the mighty hand of God, so that he may exalt you at the proper time."[15]

From these verses, it's clear that it is our job to humble ourselves. We not only have the ability to cultivate humility but the responsibility to do it. Equally important, it is not our job to try to humble other people. It is not our job to try to cut people down to size or to humiliate them, hoping that will keep them humble. We live in a world where this is unfortunately a common practice, especially on social media, but the Lord calls us to humble ourselves, not to keep each other humble.

We not only have the ability to cultivate humility but the responsibility to do it.

Furthermore, I would imagine that we have to keep humbling ourselves because there's a danger we might forget who exalted us and why. If God chooses to exalt us, it will always be for his glory, not ours. In a world obsessed with building platforms, brands, and increasing our influence and reach, God takes all the stress and striving out of it for us. He says that the way up is down. We don't have to try to hustle, promote, build, and strive; we simply need to humble ourselves.

A Lesson in Humility

There is no doubt that we will be humbled as we find ourselves in humbling positions throughout life, but the call to follow Christ and humble ourselves is about so much more than merely reacting or responding to what happens to us. We are called to pursue humility, and one way we do that, very practically, is by putting ourselves in a position to learn, to grow, and to be stretched beyond our comfort, strength, expertise, and status quo.

I remember when I turned fifty. I wanted to continue being fruitful in the second half of my life. But as I looked at how rapidly the world was changing and all that was happening in my daughters' generation, I had to be humble enough to realize that I would need more training, skills, and development. So even though I was leading a global ministry, I decided to go back to school. Because I wanted to keep learning and growing, I started a masters in evangelism and leadership at Wheaton College. I also prefer to do things in community rather than alone, so I decided to launch Propel Cohorts in partnership with Wheaton, where I could study with and learn from other women. It was one of the best experiences of my life, and four years later I graduated with the first cohort to complete the program. I am committed to being a lifelong learner so I can continue to be fruitful in doing what I'm called to do.

I wish I could tell you it was easy from the start, but it was far from it. As much as it was a privilege to further my education, it was equally a lesson in humility. I remember the first day I showed up for class, I felt so out of place. Most of my classmates were in their twenties and thirties and not too many years out of school. But for me, it had been decades since I'd been in a classroom.

When the professor passed out the syllabus and went over all that we needed to know for turning in assignments, I felt overwhelmed. I couldn't get over how much there was to learn before I could start learning what I had come to school to learn. In other words, there was software to master, portals with passwords to understand, and virtual libraries to navigate. I never would have made it without my daughters helping me repeatedly. Like so many kids, they had grown up attending school with the latest technology. Their phones were loaded with all the apps and shortcuts that schools often use today. With their help, I eventually built an entirely new set of skills.

It was a humbling experience to realize that while I might have felt at the top of my game and proficient in many areas of my life, when it came to grad school assignments, I was a beginner—and it was so uncomfortable. Still, I wanted to keep moving forward, so I chose to be willing to grow, willing to be curious, willing to be a novice again, willing to learn, willing to be challenged, willing to change, willing to be stretched, willing to potentially fail, willing to be uncomfortable. I know from experience that the moment we think we've arrived, we'll find ourselves moving out of humility and into a place we don't really want to be.

God has so many plans and purposes for our lives—so much he wants us to fulfill. Grad school was one thing he wanted me to accomplish, and now that it is behind me, I know there is so much more ahead of me. And I know the way forward is to keep walking in humility. It was James who wrote, "God resists the proud but gives grace to the humble."[16]

It's when we walk in humility that the doors to God's future plans for us open. It's when we walk in humility that we stay in step with him and all that he wants to do in us and through us. It's when we walk in humility that we have the greatest impact on those around us—particularly the ones yet to be grafted into the family of God. I mean, let's face it, no one likes a know-it-all, and contrary to how much we think we know or how educated we might be, no one knows it all but God alone.

I don't think a lost world is impressed by how much we think we know. I think that a posture of humility and a willingness to listen, learn, and be taught is compelling and attractive to people—along with an acknowledgment that many things are uncertain and as much a mystery to us as followers of Christ as they might be to others. Our job is not to impress people with how much we know, or how accomplished we might be, or how capable we may be; our job is to lead people to the only One who is truly great and who knows the beginning from the end and everything in between.

Humility Brings Us Great Joy

In our world of "self," being humble is not exactly something everyone is clamoring to become. Whether it's the pressure to posture for attention, positions, or opportunities at work or the self-promotion required of influencers on social media, most everywhere we look we're more likely to see people lifting themselves up rather than lifting others up. I don't imagine everyone feels the need to compete to get ahead, but we live in a world where it can often feel necessary. Still, God told us to humble ourselves. Jesus demonstrated humility for us; it's something we should all want to emulate. After all, we want to become more like Christ—always—and Jesus was definitely humble.

In Matthew 11, when Jesus invited the people who were weary and burdened to come to him to find rest for their souls, he described himself as "lowly and humble in heart."[17] The word translated as *lowly* in this verse is the Greek word *tapeinós*, while the word translated as *humble* is *tapeinóō*, which means to be "lowly in spirit."[18] This is why some translations describe Jesus's attitude as lowly in spirit. He came low—to earth from heaven—to make a way for us to have a relationship with his heavenly Father, to be grafted into his kingdom. That was his attitude, his demeanor, his mission, and his posture—and that's how we're to walk spiritually on this earth as well.

This is what came to mind on one of my trips to an olive farm, where I saw the branches of the trees heavy with fruit. The limbs with the most olives were low to the ground. The ones with less fruit were still up high. While I understand the natural reasons for the limbs laden with fruit to be almost touching the ground, I couldn't help but think about Jesus and his posture. I thought of him coming down to earth, being lowly in spirit, taking on the form of a servant and all the fruit this produced—people grafted into his family, people saved by grace, people abiding in him, people growing in him. These people are like you and me, people he calls to walk with an attitude of humility.

It was Micah the prophet who said, "Mankind, he has told each of you what is good and what it is the LORD requires of you: to act justly, to love faithfulness, and to walk humbly with your God."[19] Imagine how much our world would change if we would simply do those three things we know to do instead of stressing out about all the things we cannot do or do not understand about God and his will for our lives.

When we walk in humility, God promises to respond to our act of obedience.

He promises that he will not forget us nor will he forget the desires of our hearts:[20] "LORD, you have heard the desire of the humble; you will strengthen their hearts. You will listen carefully."[21]

He promises to lead and guide us as we navigate through all the twists and turns we encounter: "He leads the humble in what is right and teaches them his way."[22]

He promises to hear our prayers: "And those who know Your name will put their trust in You; For You, LORD, have not forsaken those who seek You . . . He remembers them; He does not forget the cry of the humble.[23]

He promises to reward us: "For the LORD takes pleasure in his people; he adorns the humble with salvation."[24]

But that is not all! "Humility, the fear of the LORD, results in wealth, honor, and life."[25] It leads to receiving grace and wisdom[26] and experiencing true joy! "The humble will have joy after joy in the LORD."[27]

How can any of us turn down an opportunity to have more freedom and more joy? I know I can't, and I imagine neither can you. Let's set our hearts to cultivating humility in our lives so we can walk in much more of what God has for us.

LESSONS LEARNED

- God knew we would be susceptible to pride—the antitheses of humility—so he cautioned us not to boast.
- Through Jesus and his Word, God taught us that we not only have the ability to cultivate humility in our lives, but we have the responsibility to walk in humility.
- When we choose to be humble, it opens doors for so many good things God wants for us to have in our lives.

QUESTIONS FOR REFLECTION

- When we choose to humble ourselves, God promises to exalt us. Can you think of a time when you chose to walk in humility and God exalted you?
- Consider all that God promises us when we walk in humility. Is there one benefit in particular you'd like to see more of in your life?
- Out of all that Jesus did to demonstrate humility, serving others was the most recognizable. Is there someone you can serve this week, thereby demonstrating humility and becoming more like Christ?

Lesson 6

Discover Genuine Happiness

I've had the opportunity to visit many different olive farms the past few years, and to this day, I can't decide when I like best to visit. I love the trees when they are in full bloom, and I equally love when the olives have been harvested and pressed into oil—mostly because I'm convinced that I can never bring home too much olive oil.

One thing every farm owner has told me is that olive trees depend on their environment to thrive. They need to be watered consistently but not too much volume at a time. They need ample sunshine, proper pruning, and ideally, loamy soil.[1] Like all trees, they need nutrients, and those nutrients come from the soil or fertilizers. Of course, as we have already discovered, because of their hardy root system, even if something devastating happens to the trunk and foliage aboveground, the root system can revive the tree. This resilience explains why olive trees can live for thousands of years. In fact, the oldest olive trees in existence have withstood natural disasters of all kinds, and you can see the most ancient of them all in Greece, Lebanon, and Israel.[2]

One of the oldest is on the island of Crete, and it is referred to as the Olive Tree of Vouves. It's confirmed to be two thousand years old based on tree ring analysis, though some say it's between three and four thousand years old.[3] And it still produces olives!

In northern Lebanon is a cluster of sixteen ancient trees affectionally referred to as "The Sisters." They are thought to be six thousand years old, and they, too, still produce olives.[4] Locals love to tell tourists that it is from these trees the dove brought the olive branch back to Noah after the flood.[5] Of course, this can't be proven, but I imagine it gives the locals enjoyment to feed such lore to everyone who passes through.

The resiliency of olive trees is astounding. They are designed to flourish, and yet, despite their enduring vitality, like all living things, it is possible for olive trees to grow sick and begin to languish—meaning they grow weak and drained of their vitality. When an olive tree grows sick, there are often telltale signs clearly indicating they need attention. They begin to have dry, brittle yellow or brown leaves. They have spotted or wilted leaves and drop them earlier than they should in a normal year of growth. Their branches snap easily. Their trunks become mushy and cracked, particularly if they are dying. They develop conditions like fruit mummification. And if an olive tree has a fungal disease, there can be a discoloring at its base.[6]

During the past decade, in the Puglia region of Italy, nearly half a million olive trees whose gnarled trunks have stood firm through the centuries have succumbed to a bacteria spread by insects.[7] The first signs of infection were seen in the leaves—they turned brown, became crunchy, and began to fall.[8] And while many of the diseased trees died, years of experimentation have led to some success at reviving them. A regular treatment of zinc, copper, and citric acid has brought some trees back to a reproductive state. Trees thought to be dead began having green shoots coming up at the base of the trunk.

There's always hope for a season of renewed flourishing after a season of languishing.

The olive tree is a constant reminder for us all: There's always hope for a season of renewed flourishing after a season of languishing.

When We Languish Like an Olive Tree

In the same way that olive trees can languish, so can we as followers of Jesus. Yes, we are made to thrive in tough circumstances, but I imagine we'd all admit that there are times when we endure multiple hits, feeling attacked on all sides, and are left reeling and weary from it all. In such a season, it's easy to find ourselves languishing and maybe even on the verge of giving up. I imagine when David was on the run from Saul, this was where he found himself. How could he not? He spent seven years living as a fugitive, enduring physical attacks, and eventually hiding out in a cave for survival, and yet we know he definitely came out of the experience flourishing. Again, he's the one who declared, "But I am like a flourishing olive tree in the house of God; I trust in God's faithful love forever and ever."[9]

Like David, we are all human, and because of that, we are bound to face circumstances that wear us down. We may not find ourselves running for our lives, but I do not want us to lose sight of the fact that we all face times of languishing—even when we know we should be flourishing. Languishing can show up in many different ways. It can appear as a sense of fatigue, apathy, or restlessness. It can mean losing our interest in the things that typically bring us joy.[10] It can even be described as feelings of blah-ness, or meh.[11] It's not akin to burnout or depression but more like being stuck in neutral or treading water.[12] The interesting thing is that languishing isn't necessarily just one emotion but a series of them.[13]

If you've ever walked through a long illness or alongside someone fighting to be free from addiction, then you might know what it is to languish. Battling through a legal issue, weathering a divorce, or recovering from a financial setback might feel much the same. Of course, good things can cause us to languish as well. Whether we're chasing toddlers or teenagers, launching a business, getting through school, or building our careers, we can grow weary and want to quit and give up—but we don't dare, do we?

Whether we're in pursuit of our goals or walking through a difficult season, we live in a world where most everyone has become all too familiar with the feelings of languishing, particularly since 2020. *Languish* "was even identified by an organizational psychologist as the 'dominant emotion of 2021' because the word captured the weariness the world felt from pivoting over and over."[14]

When it comes to our lives spiritually, languishing is just as real. It can show up as feelings of spiritual stagnation or emptiness.[15] It can leave us with an uneasy heart or an unquiet mind.[16] It can cause us to have a sense of being weary, passionless, jaded, aimless, or joyless.[17] I know I've felt all of these emotions at different times in my four decades of following Jesus.

In fact, I recently came out of a period of languishing after dealing with the sudden loss of a friendship that was very dear to me. It left me feeling deeply hurt, wounded, and rejected. I was so blindsided by the abrupt ending that I spent months replaying what I could have said and done differently, wondering why my friend was willing to walk away, including how she could walk away without taking responsibility for how much she had hurt me. And during all those months, I kept doing everything that needed to be done in my external world, and it was producing such fruitfulness. To look at my ministry life, you would agree with me that everything was flourishing, but in my heart and soul I was wilting like an olive tree that had lost its vitality.

I was the same tree but in a different season. My roots still ran deep. My trunk was strong. My branches were connected. But despite my best efforts, my leaves were starting to sail to the ground. I didn't feel as green and flourishing—not by a long shot.

I remember the day it all came to a tipping point. I was walking along the beach during a lunch break at a conference where I was the keynote speaker. My heart was utterly broken, and the tears wouldn't stop. I was physically exhausted, and I knew I needed to take a pause and do whatever it took to get back to a place of flourishing, even though at the time I'm not even sure I really believed it was possible. A verse from the Psalms became my hourly prayer: "Be gracious to me, O LORD, for I am languishing; heal me, O LORD, for my bones are troubled."[18]

God has indeed been gracious to me, and he has healed me,

but it was definitely a journey. I am so grateful for the patience and kindness of God—he is so tender and merciful. He promises each one of us: "For I will [fully] satisfy the weary soul, and I will replenish every languishing and sorrowful person."[19]

When we're languishing, it's rarely an easy season; it's typically not pretty, but pressing through such a time is what helps us become more resilient. If we'll hang in there with God through the process, he will be our spiritual equivalent of zinc, copper, and citric acid. He has a habit of bringing dead things back to life by the power of his Spirit. God is full of resurrection life, and he lives inside us.[20] "And if the Spirit of him who raised Jesus from the dead lives in you, then he who raised Christ from the dead will also bring your mortal bodies to life through his Spirit who lives in you."[21] Because of this truth, I am never without hope when I am languishing . . . and neither are you.

God Wants Even More for Us

Beyond recovering from languishing, there is flourishing, and I believe God wants us to experience and testify to that truth just like David was able to do! I don't know what flourishing might look like in your life, but for me it comes with feelings of being present, alive, and full of joy. It comes with a white-hot passion in my heart for God. It comes with laughter and a motivation to get out and hike, bike, run, and soak up the waves of the ocean. It comes with good health and physical strength. It comes with appreciating all the years Nick and I have been happily married. It comes with captivating conversations with my daughters and long chats with friends. It comes with rest and quiet moments with God, with frequent views of sunrises and sunsets. When I'm flourishing, I feel vibrant and thriving in most every area of my life. What's more, and this may surprise you, I feel completely happy, something God wants for all of us.

That's right. God not only wants to resurrect us and replenish us—to get us from languishing to flourishing again—but he goes so far as to want us happy. How can we be certain of this? Because the meaning of *flourishing* includes being happy,[22] and because God takes the initiative to talk about being happy numerous times in his Word. The first verse of Psalm 128, for example, clearly says, "How happy is everyone who fears the Lord, who walks in his ways!"

We all want to be happy, don't we? I mean, who wants to be miserable? Besides, being happy comes with loads of benefits. When people are happy they typically have a lower heart rate, lower blood pressure, less stress, and as a result, a much longer life expectancy.[23] When people are happy, it can lead to a better immune system and a willingness to exercise and better care for themselves. When people are happy, they are more productive, innovative, and engaged.[24] They are more generous—with their time, talents, and treasure. They even experience better relationships. There's really no downside to being happy, is there?

It's no wonder people are obsessed with pursuing happiness wherever they can, especially when you take into consideration that feelings of being overwhelmed, anxious, stressed, discontent, and depressed are at an all-time high in our world. Knowing this, it's not hard to understand why people look for happiness in relationships, achievements, possessions, careers, sports, hobbies, or traveling. Of course, God has no problem with us going on a bucket-list trip or joining a community softball team or taking up a new interest. But most of the things we might pursue can only bring us moments or seasons of happiness that inevitably come to an end—typically when the reality of the broken world we live in comes crashing down on us.

The good news is, in our internal world, in a spiritual context, we have the ability to be happy even when aspects of our external world are not ideal. Of course, I am saying this in the context of us living our normal everyday lives and dealing with all the inconveniences we sometimes experience—waiting in long lines, not getting a delivery we expected, having a meal we ordered prepared incorrectly, missing a flight, and so forth. The point is that when our happiness is rooted in God, we can have a bad day and still be happy!

> In our internal world, in a spiritual context, we have the ability to be happy even when aspects of our external world are not ideal.

I'm not saying that when we face deep disappointment, gut-wrenching heartache, sorrow, loss, or tragedy, God expects us to put a smile on our face and pretend to be happy. No, not at all. There are times when we need to grieve and the pain-filled tears we cry leave no room for happiness. Certainly in instances of war, genocide, abuse, domestic violence, natural disasters, and other such tragedies and injustices, happiness is obviously not the appropriate response or goal.

But in the midst of all that goes on in a typical day, God wants us to live with happiness in our hearts and our emotions—not fakeness, denial, or superficiality but hope and vitality. Because we have Jesus. Because we have the one who is the same yesterday, today, and forever.[25] Because we have the one in whom all things are possible.[26] Because we are rooted, resilient, and fruitful in him.

If you find this idea uncomfortable or feel yourself resisting it, I understand. Please hang with me. For some, this might sound polar opposite to what we think of as our personality, causing us to object straightaway. For others, we may see pursuing being happy as selfish, shallow, or unspiritual. For example, if we were raised in a strict religious tradition, we may view God as some kind of cosmic killjoy and find it hard to believe he cares about our happiness—but he most definitely does. He wants us flourishing, and to flourish is to be happy!

Despite how the idea may make us feel, Psalm 128 shows us that it is not only spiritual to desire to be happy but it is a part of our spiritual inheritance as children of God. Just as much as God wants us to experience forgiveness, love, acceptance, safety, security, peace, contentment, and everything else that we might readily embrace, he also wants us to experience happiness.

I'm well aware that the psalmist said we'd be happy if we fear the Lord and walk in his ways. Yes, there is a condition, but it is a good condition—especially if we fully understand what it is to fear the Lord. Fearing God, biblically, does not mean to be scared of God, thinking he's whimsical or unreliable. God is not those things. He's faithful, steadfast, and trustworthy. He is a gracious, loving, merciful, and compassionate Father who does only what is good for us. Psalm 119:68 says of God, "You are good, and you do what is good."

To fear the Lord is to take him seriously, to reverence and

respect him deeply, to honor him greatly, and to live with him as the ultimate authority in our lives. And when we do, we find happiness. Psalm 34:8–9 says, "Taste and see that the LORD is good. How happy is the person who takes refuge in him! You who are his holy ones, fear the LORD, for those who fear him lack nothing." Fearing God leads to happiness, because when we fear God, we obey God, and when we obey God, we turn from sin and don't live with its anxiety, weight, and consequences. As Proverbs 28:14 says, "Happy is the one who is always reverent, but one who hardens his heart falls into trouble."

If we will consciously fear the Lord, then everything promised in Psalm 128 is available to us. That's the only stipulation. What's more, the next couple of verses in Psalm 128 go on to describe the blessings of God that come with fearing him: "You will surely eat what your hands have worked for. You will be happy, and it will go well for you. Your wife will be like a fruitful vine within your house, your children, like young olive trees around your table."[27]

I love how God so plainly spells it out for us: "You will be happy, and it will go well for you." When God emphatically says something like this in his Word, we call it a promise, and a promise is something we can trust and rely on. What's more, I particularly love that this passage includes another verse comparing us to olive trees. It says that our children will be like young olive trees around our table.

There's nothing Nick and I enjoy more than time with our girls. Their youthful vitality and interesting perspectives are part of what makes us happy! We love sitting around the dinner table with them while they make us think or make us laugh until our sides hurt.

Now, if you don't have children, that does not mean you are excluded from the blessings God mentions in this verse. The psalmist talks about the blessing of family because in ancient Israel it was expected that everyone would be married and have children. But if that is not the path your life has taken, I want to remind you of a few things.

First, we have all been adopted into the family of God, and there's a seat at the table for every one of us. If marriage and children were a prerequisite for God's blessings, then Jesus would not have qualified because he was never married nor did he have any children.

Second, the happy life, the blessed life, or the flourishing life has to do with the everyday details of our lives: our work, our food, our homes, and our families. That is the bigger point being made with these verses. God cares about our well-being in every area of our lives. That doesn't mean, of course, that we should expect a problem-free life; it does mean that whatever life throws our way, we have Jesus, we're looking to Jesus, and we're putting our trust in Jesus. True contentment and happiness are ultimately found in enjoying God himself, who remains ever faithful to each of us every single day.

LESSONS LEARNED

- There's always hope for a season of renewed flourishing after a season of languishing.
- When we're languishing, if we hang in there with God, he will be our spiritual equivalent of zinc, copper, and citric acid. He has a habit of bringing dead things back to life by the power of his Spirit.
- God not only wants to resurrect us and replenish us—to get us from languishing to flourishing again— but he goes so far as to want us happy.

QUESTIONS FOR REFLECTION

- If you are in a season of languishing, what steps can you take toward flourishing?
- Do you struggle with the idea that God wants you to be happy? Why?
- In what areas can you trust Jesus more so you can enjoy more happiness?

Lesson 7

Tap Into the Endless Oil of the Holy Spirit

It hadn't been long since Nick and I crossed the border from Italy into Slovenia when I caught sight of the first olive farm. The brilliant blue of the Adriatic Sea stretched to our right, and terraced up the hillside on our left were endless rows of olive trees. It was all so breathtaking that I wasn't sure whether to look to the left or the right, and at first I found myself darting back and forth. But we'd come for the olive trees, so that's where I landed. There had to be hundreds of them dancing in the breeze, as if they were as excited as I was. Nick and I were able to get away for a few days, just the two of us, and having heard about Slovenia's world-famous olive oil, I couldn't wait to taste it.

The olive trees in Slovenia are some of the northernmost in the world, and though the small country is not known as a major olive oil producer like Spain, Italy, or Greece, its olive oil is ranked as some of the best in the world. A number of their producers have won awards at prestigious competitions such as the New York International Olive Oil Competition.[1] And that's saying a lot, as there are only about forty olive farms along the roughly eighteen miles of coastline that are registered and producing premium extra-virgin olive oil.[2] They are all typically family owned and operated and—at most—have one thousand trees each. Some of the trees are as old as one hundred years, having been planted by previous generations and only rediscovered in the past thirty years along overgrown terraces. Together with trees planted in recent decades, they make up the blend of olives used to make Slovenia's award-winning olive oil.

Finding the entrance to a farm, we wound our way to their processing center where we finally got a taste of their olive oil. I'll admit it was like no other I've ever had. Strong. Robust. Memorable. Fruity. Bitter. Spicy. All at once! I wanted to bring home a crate of it, but then again, I always want to bring home a crate of most every olive oil I try. I love dousing my favorite foods with a healthy splash, and when it's an oil full of flavor like Slovenia's, well, I'm apt to douse a little more.

Of all the olives harvested in the world, about 80 percent are pressed for oil and the remaining 20 percent are eaten as table olives.[3] Historically, olive oil has been used for everything from sautéing to baking to cosmetics to medicine. I remember my mum using it in our home to oil everything from her hands to squeaky hinges to her cutting board. The uses seem endless and are fascinating. But what's even more interesting to me are the ways that olive oil is used in the Bible, particularly for anointing. On many occasions we read of people, places, or things having oil poured on them and that act being referred to as anointing the person, place, or thing. But why were things anointed, and what was the significance?

Certainly anointing someone or something served to send a message—that the person or thing was set apart for the Lord and his service, that the person or thing was his and to be used for his purposes. Moses poured olive oil on Aaron when he was consecrated as the first high priest.[4] Jacob anointed a rock to consecrate it and mark it as a place belonging to the Lord.[5] The priests anointed the furniture in the tabernacle to consecrate them and set them apart as the Lord's.[6] And when kings, priests, and prophets entered into the Lord's service, we often read of them being anointed with oil as a demonstration and declaration of their consecration to God and his purposes.

Anointing with oil sent a message. It signaled that someone or something was set apart *for* him. But that wasn't—and isn't—the only reality that anointing represented or conveyed in Scripture. For some people, when they were anointed with olive oil, we also read about the Spirit of God coming or rushing upon them. It happened when Samuel took a flask of oil and poured it on Saul's head, anointing him as king.[7] It happened again when Samuel anointed David as the next king, though he was still a shepherd boy.[8] In both instances the Holy Spirit supplied them each with his presence and his power for service.

This is so significant! By having anointing with oil signify both the setting apart and the Holy Spirit being the source for ministry, God was making a critical point: Ministry *for* him is ministry that is done *with* him through continual reliance upon him, his power, and his presence. Anything else is not ministry—it's activity.

> Ministry *for* him is ministry that is done *with* him through continual reliance upon him, his power, and his presence.

When Zechariah had a dream about two olive trees endlessly pouring olive oil into two lampstands—so they burned brightly and the light in the tabernacle never went out—the olive oil represented the endless supply of the oil of the Holy Spirit. An angel interpreted the dream saying, "'Not by strength or by might, but by my Spirit,' says the LORD."[9] The angel's explanation was a message for us all in every sphere of our lives: The oil of the Holy Spirit burning bright in us is what fills our tank and keeps us going strong. Without him, without ongoing reliance on him, we will find ourselves empty from all our activity and all that life constantly throws at us—and we will lose resiliency.

There are and always will be challenges to our faith and to all that God has called us to do. There are and always will be disappointments, disruptions, and disillusionments. There are and always will be reasons to grow weary in it all, to want to stop and quit. We cannot possibly fulfill a supernatural calling with our natural strength, gifts, talents, resources, or abilities. God himself has ensured that we need him to do the very things he has called us to do. Whether we're raising our kids, working hard at our jobs, needing to forgive someone, loving our neighbors or our enemies, or doing our best to be a good spouse, a good parent, or a good friend, we need the power of the Holy Spirit to empower, strengthen, and sustain us.

Jesus modeled this life of dependence for us. He, too, was anointed—not with oil, but with the Holy Spirit himself.[10]

Jesus's name tells us he was anointed. In Scripture he is referred to both as *Jesus* and *Jesus Christ*. *Jesus* is his given name, the one the angel Gabriel announced to Mary. It's what his mother called him. *Christ* is his title, not his surname, and it is a derivative of *Christos*, a Greek word that means "the anointed one." The Hebrew word meaning the same thing is *Mashiach*, or as we know it, *Messiah*.[11] Jesus is the Christ, the Son of the living God, the anointed one.[12]

But beyond that, when John the Baptist baptized Jesus in the Jordan River, Jesus came up out of the water and the Holy Spirit descended on him like a dove.[13] This illustrated that Jesus never did anything apart from the Spirit.

And Jesus testified to the Holy Spirit's anointing. In his very first recorded sermon, he explained that his anointing was for service and not for status, declaring that, "The Spirit of the Lord is on me, because he has anointed me to preach good news to the poor. He has sent me to proclaim release to the captives and recovery of sight to the blind, to set free the oppressed, to proclaim the year of the Lord's favor."[14]

Jesus was aware of and affirmed the significance of the anointing of the Holy Spirit. Are we doing the same today? Are we recognizing that it's the Holy Spirit who helps us flourish and be resilient and fruitful during our time on this earth?

The Holy Spirit Our Anointing

Even in our day we see people anointed. If you live in a nation with a monarchy, for example, then you possibly understand what it is to have someone anointed as a king or queen. Having grown up in Australia and married a man with a British passport, I've always found monarchies fascinating. In 2023, when the Church of England conducted the coronation of King Charles III, more than twenty million viewers watched, including me.[15] If you tuned in, then you might have noticed the part of the coronation ceremony when King Charles III was anointed, which symbolized the gift of the Holy Spirit and the monarch's divine election.[16] You couldn't see it when it happened because the screens placed around the king concealed him from view, but the archbishop anointed the king's hands, breast, and head with holy oil—which was olive oil. And not just any olive oil. According to Buckingham Palace, the olive oil, or *chrism* as it was referred to for the coronation, was produced from olives grown on the Mount of Olives—the same place where Jesus prayed in the Garden of Gethsemane.[17] It was consecrated in Jerusalem and based on the same ingredients as the oil used in the 1953 coronation of Queen Elizabeth II—a formula used for hundreds of years.[18] It is known to contain ambergris, orange flowers, roses, jasmine, and cinnamon, though the exact formula is a well-kept secret.

If you watched the coronation, then maybe you found this part of the ceremony especially intriguing, since the idea of being anointed today can come with any number of interpretations—with or without oil. Depending on your church background, the idea of anointing may be something you've heard a lot about, or it may be something you've heard practically nothing about. And if you've heard of it at all, you've probably heard it spoken of in different ways.

In some streams of the church, it's a common practice to anoint people with physical oil when they're baptized, confirmed, given a blessing, prayed over for healing, or administered last rites. In other streams of the church, it's not necessarily about being anointed with physical oil but about a spiritual description.

For example, in some circles, someone being "anointed" can be used almost like a status description of importance. In other circles, an anointing is spoken of as something someone has, almost as though it's a possession. In still other circles, the idea of being anointed can be so sought and prized that it becomes a source of idolatry, jealousy, and competition. Or it can be left completely unmentioned, signaling that it is an irrelevant topic for our lives and generation.

> We are also designed to walk and serve in the power of the Spirit.

But anointing wasn't irrelevant for Jesus. And it isn't irrelevant for us. We are set apart for God.[19] But we are also designed to walk and serve in the power of the Spirit as we obey him and depend on him to do through us what we cannot do on our own.[20] We don't want to go to God in the morning and then go off on our own. That's activity, not ministry. We want to be anointed, set apart for, and sourced by the Spirit as we stay in step with him. Anointing is not something reserved for the elite, special troops of Christianity. It is something we should acknowledge, seek to understand, and consciously walk in. It's something we all need in our everyday lives. We need who he is. We need to receive from who he is. And we need to respond to who he is if he's going to be our source to flourish, grow more resilient, and be fruitful. So who is he?

The Holy Spirit Our Counselor

The Holy Spirit has always been present, even since before what we might consider to be the beginning of time, but he's only been in us and with us in the special way he is today since Jesus ascended into heaven.[21]

Before Jesus left this earth, he promised to send us a helper—the Holy Spirit—who is the third person of the Trinity. When I say this, I do not want you to think of the Godhead as having a hierarchy like Olympic medalists: God the Father is the gold medalist, Jesus the Son is the silver medalist, and the Holy Spirit is the bronze medalist. Granted, the Trinity is a mystery and not easy to comprehend with our natural minds, but each member of the Trinity is equally God—not a lesser or secondary version of the other. Just like God the Father sent Jesus to earth, Jesus sent the Holy Spirit: "When the Counselor comes, the one I will send to you from the Father—the Spirit of truth who proceeds from the Father—he will testify about me."[22]

Forty days after Jesus's resurrection, he ascended into heaven. Ten days after that, the Holy Spirit came. His coming occurred in the Upper Room, the place when the apostles, disciples, and key figures in Jesus's life—including his mother, Mary—were all gathered. You're probably familiar with the dramatic event surrounding Pentecost:

> Suddenly a sound like that of a violent rushing wind came from heaven, and it filled the whole house where they were staying. They saw tongues like flames of fire that separated and rested on each one of them. Then they were all filled with the Holy Spirit and began to speak in different tongues, as the Spirit enabled them.[23]

The significance of this one moment in time forever changed the way the early Christians lived their spiritual lives and evangelized the world. They were now filled with God's Spirit internally, and they had consistent access to that Spirit to empower them.

Even more revealing is that the Holy Spirit's name in the original Greek is *paraklētos,* a word used in John 14:26 that has a range of meanings.[24] While most translations use only one word for *paraklētos,* The Amplified Bible lists several:

> But the Comforter (Counselor, Helper, Intercessor, Advocate, Strengthener, Standby), the Holy Spirit, Whom the Father will send in My name [in My place, to represent Me and act on My behalf], He will teach you all things. And He will cause you to recall (will remind you of, bring to your remembrance) everything I have told you.[25]

The Holy Spirit's name reveals who he is—and many of the things he does for us.

He strengthens us with a kind of comfort no human can.[26]
He leads us in what it is God wants us to do.[27]
He speaks to, cautions, and directs us.[28]
He teaches us and reminds us of what Jesus said.[29]
He leads and empowers us in prayer.[30]
He gives us godly wisdom.[31]

Like God the Father and God the Son, the Holy Spirit—depicted as olive oil in Zechariah's dream and revealed to us throughout Scripture—is endless. And he's available to us every minute of every day.

Perhaps you have never considered the Holy Spirit to be a

person with such qualities. Growing up in the Greek Orthodox Church, I didn't. I do remember hearing the Holy Spirit mentioned when we recited the Nicene Creed in our liturgy, but I must confess I truly thought that when people referred to the Holy Ghost, he was something more like a literal ghost or some other spirit depicted in a movie. I had no idea he was a person to be known or that he was available to help me live how God had called me to live 24/7 on this earth.

After I became a fully devoted follower of Jesus in my early twenties, I began to acknowledge the third person of the Trinity in my prayer life and in my spiritual practices as a way to make space for him in my mind, in my heart, and in my everyday life. After reading a book about the Holy Spirit, I remember going through a season where I would wake up every morning and the first thing I'd say was, "Good morning, Holy Spirit." At first it felt uncomfortable, weird even. But the more I acknowledged him, the more I invited him into my thoughts, the more I asked for his help and guidance and strength, the more I saw him show up. I wasn't replacing Jesus or God the Father with the Holy Spirit; I was including him. I was relating to him, something I'd never done.

And as I did, I not only saw him as God, because that's who he is, I also began experiencing him as my personal *paraklētos*. I developed a rhythm of including him in my decisions that continues to this day. Instead of running ahead of him, I consistently ask him to help me with my relationships, conversations, finances, marriage, parenting, planning, messages, posting on social media, taking on new projects—I could go on and on. He is my helper and my friend, and he is so much smarter than I am. I can't tell you the number of times in a twenty-four-hour period that I turn to the Holy Spirit in prayer, because I need him. Because I need his endless supply of oil. And if I were able to sit down and enjoy a cup of coffee with you, then I imagine we'd discover that you do too.

LESSONS LEARNED

- The oil of the Holy Spirit burning bright in us is what fills our tank and keeps us going strong, flourishing, serving, and producing fruit. Without ongoing reliance on him, we will find ourselves empty from all our activity and all that life constantly throws at us.
- Being anointed means we are set apart for God. But we are also designed to walk and serve in the power of the Spirit as we obey him and depend on him to do through us what we cannot do on our own.
- The anointing of the Holy Spirit is something we should acknowledge, seek to understand, and consciously walk in. We need the ministry of the Holy Spirit in our everyday lives.

QUESTIONS FOR REFLECTION

- Jesus affirmed the significance of the anointing of the Holy Spirit. Are you doing the same today?
- The Holy Spirit is the third person of the Trinity and someone we are to relate to every day. Is this something you're doing now? How can you begin acknowledging him in your life?
- In what ways can you begin leaning into the Holy Spirit as your own personal *paraklētos*?

Lesson 8

Follow the Holy Spirit Your Guide

When Nick and I visited Slovenia in search of more olive trees and to taste their world-famous olive oil, I convinced him that we should hike one of the iconic chain of lakes trails that leads up to Mount Triglav, the most beloved mountain in the country. It's located inside the 340 square miles of Mount Triglav National Park, and the trails promise picturesque views of meadows, wildflowers, a spruce forest, and snowcapped peaks towering above it all—plus seven pristine, clear blue lakes. Those are the must-see gems of the trip.

I chose the path through the Seven Lakes Valley that starts at Planina Blato. It's 17.5 miles from start to finish, and the first four hours are straight up a 4,400-foot incline.[1] I knew it would be difficult to traverse and would test my endurance as well as all my hiking skills, but every review I read promised the trek would be more than worth it, so I was all in.[2]

We drove to the park entrance early, as parking was only available on the roadside leading to the trail and it filled quickly. We were so glad we arrived early, because soon after we parked and began walking toward the trailhead, we heard from other hikers that the park stopped all access because there were no more parking spaces available.

Stopping to read a sign updating hikers about the latest trail conditions, I felt reassured that we were about to have the best day. When in a foreign country, I would normally hire a guide to lead us on such a long hike. They're familiar with the trails, fluent in the language, and have experience that could prove useful should anything go wrong. But I felt that I had done my research and really wanted to impress Nick with my exceptional hiking skills. I planned to be his guide on this hike, even though I had never been on this particular trail—or, for that matter, in this country. What could possibly go wrong?

I wish I could tell you it turned out to be a stellar day and that everything went according to plan just as I imagined but that would not be true. The views we did get to see didn't disappoint, but we got lost on the way and missed every one of the seven lakes. I didn't realize the snow hadn't melted near the top of the mountains, and we didn't have ice cleats for our boots. We tried to walk across the snow, but I slipped and almost fell off a ledge.

As much as I didn't want to admit defeat, if I wanted to stay alive I had to accept that we needed to go back down the way we had come—though that meant missing all the spectacular sights we had set out to see. I was devastated. Had we only secured a guide, he or she would have told us to take a different trail. Then we would have gotten to see all seven of the lakes. I wouldn't have wasted all my energy. I wouldn't have been disappointed. I wouldn't have almost died. A guide would have made all the difference.

The Holy Spirit Our Truth

When I first started seriously hiking during the global pandemic of 2020, my friend Dawn was my guide. She taught me all the basics—what kind of shoes to wear, what kind of clothing to wear, what kind of poles to buy, and how to prepare my body physically in the days leading up to a big hike. She checked the weather in advance and adjusted our plans accordingly. And once we hit a trail, she led the way because that's what a guide does. A *guide* "provides someone with *guiding* information."[3]

On every hike Dawn walked ahead of me to watch for danger and warn me what missteps to avoid and where to stabilize my footing. She carried our first aid kit for all the scrapes, bruises, and injuries I now know come with hiking. She pointed out all the flora and wildlife so I wouldn't miss any of it. She knew all the best places to stop and rest and take in the views—so I didn't overexert myself and want to quit. She told me when to stop and eat, whether I thought I needed to or not. She told me when to hydrate and how much to drink, even when I wasn't thirsty. She made sure I stayed on the right trail and didn't get lost, particularly when we came to a fork where I could have gone left or right. She made sure I reached the summit of every mountain and didn't miss the best part of the journey. Had Nick and I had Dawn with us in Slovenia—or someone equally qualified—it would have transformed our entire experience.

If you've ever taken a guided tour through a museum, a zoo, a historical landmark, or some other point of interest, then you know the value of a guide. They know all the facts. They are your go-to for all your questions. They know the best places to eat. They know where the nearest restrooms are. They ensure your safety, and if you're in a part of the world that doesn't speak your language, they serve as your interpreter. To get the most out of any trip, a guide is essential.

I'm so glad that, when it comes to our journey, when it comes to all the adventures of our life in Christ, we don't have to—and aren't designed to—be our own guide. We don't have to find our way forward as best we can. Quite the contrary. God has given us our very own personal guide; he's given us the Holy Spirit. "When the Spirit of truth comes, he will guide you into all the truth."[4]

The Holy Spirit is in us and with us to help us navigate the inevitable twists, turns, trials, temptations, and tribulations of living in this world—so we continue to flourish.[5] He has been given to us to provide us with information—but not just any information. He is the Spirit of truth, so he leads and guides us into all the truth; he will never, never lead us into one single degree of darkness or deception.[6]

> The Holy Spirit is in us and with us to help us navigate the inevitable twists, turns, trials, temptations, and tribulations of living in this world—so we continue to flourish.

I find this so comforting because we live in an age where truth is relative, where chaos and confusion are everywhere, where people claim to have their own truth. Our newsfeeds are flooded with fake news, and with AI we don't even know what is real anymore.

If we are to live the faith-filled, purpose-driven life God has called us to live, we need to know what is true—and what is not. We need to know who to really trust—and who not to trust. We need to know where to go—and where not to go. We need to know what to think—and what not to think. We need to know what to believe—and what not to believe. We desperately need a guide!

From the day we truly surrender our lives to Jesus, the Holy Spirit actively guides us, whether we recognize him at work in our lives or not. In fact, it's the Holy Spirit who initially draws us all into a relationship with Jesus,[7] and it's the Holy Spirit who is supposed to guide us for the rest of our spiritual journey. In Isaiah he is described as "a Spirit of wisdom and understanding, a Spirit of counsel and strength, a Spirit of knowledge and of the fear of the Lord."[8] He literally knows everything we need to know, and he has the wisdom to help us skillfully apply his guidance. To be sure we don't miss that guidance, we need to develop a relationship with him—one where we practice speaking directly to him in prayer, asking for his help, and then actively listening for his response.

The Holy Spirit Our Lead

I'll admit that following a guide up a mountain can be far easier than following our guide the Holy Spirit, mostly because we can't see or audibly hear him like we can another person. Still, like the Holy Spirit did with Paul and other members of the early church, he's supposed to show us the way, and we're supposed to follow his lead.[9]

So how do we do that? How do we recognize when it's him leading us?

According to Scripture there's not one way but multiple ways. But none of those ways contradict what God says in the Bible because that is the primary way the Holy Spirit speaks to us. Beyond that we know he speaks through dreams, visions, and prophecies. He speaks with what's called "the inner witness," something we understand from Romans 8:16: "The Spirit himself bears witness with our spirit that we are children of God."[10] He speaks through our discernment, our thoughts, and through wisdom from the Word. Proverbs is a book in the Bible that is full of his wisdom. He speaks through messages and from mature and trusted leaders and friends. He even speaks through signs, as it's one of the ways he confirms God's Word.[11] Every time I board a flight at a gate labeled A21, I just smile. Soon after we decided to start The A21 Campaign to fight human trafficking, I boarded a flight at a gate numbered A21. To me it was sign; it served as a confirmation that I was heading in the right direction.

If you are starting to feel uncomfortable with all that I'm saying or having flashbacks to all the spiritual weirdness you've encountered, I get it. I recognize why you might be hesitant and wary of delving into these waters. So much damage has been done in the name of God. I get that it's quite possible you have been hurt, disappointed, and left utterly confused because someone said they were being guided by the Holy Spirit when the results that ensued clearly showed they were not. If what they said, suggested, or did couldn't be grounded in God's Word, which includes his principles, then it's safe to say they were not being guided by the Holy Spirit. And I'm deeply sorry for how their misguidedness wounded you and for all the years you've possibly had to work through that. I've been there, and perhaps like you, I've somewhat developed a thick skin when it comes to listening to people who emphatically believe they are being guided by the Holy Spirit with no room for human error. I've also taken to heart the idea that it would be better if we were more careful about linking what we feel and what we sense with what we think God is saying.

I'll never forget a young woman once telling me in a church service that the Holy Spirit told her the worship leader was going to be her husband. I didn't want to burst her bubble, but I couldn't help myself. I immediately blurted out, "Well, you might want to run that by his wife." The Holy Spirit would never guide a woman to take another woman's husband. The seventh commandment makes it very clear: "Do not commit adultery."[12]

If you're like me, then experiences like this have given you an aversion to listening to someone who starts a sentence with the words, "God said." I just can't help but take whatever follows with a grain of salt, especially if it's from a person who says "God said" one thing one day, something completely different the next day, and possibly something else the next. If God really changed his mind that much, if he were truly that indecisive, how would we ever trust him? I imagine if he were like that then we'd all be suffering from spiritual whiplash and have zero courage to step out in faith about anything.

I'm grateful that the Word says he changes not; that he's the same yesterday, today, and forevermore; that we can trust him with all our hearts, souls, and minds; that if God did indeed say it or promise it, then he will do it.[13]

I know in my marriage and parenting and in leading our global team, I avoid starting a conversation with "God said," because how is anyone supposed to respond to that? It immediately overpowers them. If I were to say to one of my daughters, "God said you cannot go to that school," for example, then I would completely disempower them from being able to feel like they could express their ideas to me—including how the Holy Spirit might be guiding them. It would be so irresponsible of me. Besides, I could be wrong. And I need their input so we can collaboratively make the best decision. I'm just as much in my family's lives, and in my team's lives, to learn from them as they are to learn from me. I want my team members to feel they can bring me all the guidance they're getting from the Holy Spirit. It's part of why they're on our team.

So very practically, how do I honor God's speaking and invite others to be a part of hearing and discerning what he is saying? It's through inquiring prayer. Personal inquiring prayer. Corporate inquiring prayer. When we are working together to make a decision, as a family or as a team, we get with God. We ask. We humbly share what we sense God is saying, with the understanding we could be wrong, and submit that to one another for testing and confirmation.

And this should go without saying, but we should never claim that we've heard something from the Spirit to get our own way or to use as a weapon against others. Not only does that dishonor God but it causes a lot of damage.

There's no question that we all need the guidance of the Holy Spirit to flourish in life—and he wants us to bring all our cares, concerns, decisions, and questions to him to ask for his guidance.[14] That's not to say we can't make everyday decisions on our own—because God did give us the gift of choice and a mind with which to make all the choices to get through any given day.

Personally, I don't ask the Holy Spirit if I can brush my teeth or what I should eat for breakfast. I just get up and do those things. I don't ask him what I should wear—and not just because I'm most likely going to wear whatever is black and in the front of the closet anyway, but because I don't think he really cares if I want to wear a dress or jeans. Yes, he cares that it's appropriate and I care that it's appropriate, but at the end of the day, he also gives us freedom. That said, we don't want to fail to ask for his guidance regarding something he wants to lead us in because we assume it doesn't matter to him!

And whatever you think you've heard from the Holy Spirit—about anything—take it right back to him in prayer. Look for him to confirm it in his Word. Test what you think you're hearing. Test what others say they're hearing. Scripture tells us to test everything—and to hold on to what is good.[15]

I understand that none of us wants to mistake the guidance of the Holy Spirit for our own thoughts or ideas. None of us wants to wake from a dream we think is from him only to discover it was all that pizza we ate before bed. None of us wants to misinterpret coincidence or happenstance as a sign from God. None of us wants to make a wrong choice because we "listened to our hearts," because, as I mentioned in chapter 3, even our hearts aren't 100 percent reliable. "The heart is more deceitful than anything else, and incurable—who can understand it?"[16]

There is no substitute for the accuracy of the Word of God, and if we don't take the time to know the Word, then we're apt to misunderstand something to be God when it's not—no matter how many years we've walked with God. I understand that Scripture doesn't seem to cover every detail we might encounter—like whom to marry or where to move or what job to take. Still, if we turn to the Word and ask the Holy Spirit for his help in making the right decision, he will guide us. He will lead us in staying rooted, resilient, and fruitful.

How do you need the Holy Spirit to guide you today? Are you seeking how to apply a verse or passage? Are you facing a decision unlike any you've ever had to make? Are you desperate for answers on how best to mend a relationship? Are you wanting to change jobs but aren't sure it's the right timing to do so? Are you raising a child with special needs and searching for new ideas? Are you unsure how to pray for a friend who is enduring a serious illness? Are you weighing a financial decision? Whatever it is, ask the Holy Spirit for his help. Ask him to be your guide and show you the way forward.

You really don't want to wind up like Nick and I did in the Julian Alps, with me trying to play the role of guide. It makes for a good story now, but it wasn't the kind of story Nick and I had hoped to tell. All our mishaps could have been avoided if we'd taken the journey with a guide to lead us on the right path. That is the lesson of the olive tree and its oil—it depicts the ministry of the Holy Spirit to fill us and guide us on the path God has planned for us.

LESSONS LEARNED

- God has given us our very own personal guide; he's given us the Holy Spirit.
- The Holy Spirit has been given to provide us with information—but not just any information. He is the Spirit of truth, so he leads and guides us into all the truth, and he will never lead us into one single degree of darkness or deception.
- Scripture is the primary way the Holy Spirit speaks to us. Beyond that, from examples in Scripture, we know he speaks through dreams, visions, and prophecies. He speaks with what's called "the inner witness." He speaks through our discernment, our thoughts, and through wisdom from the Word. He speaks through messages and from mature and trusted leaders and friends. He even speaks through signs, as it's one of the ways he confirms God's Word.

QUESTIONS FOR REFLECTION

- How do you recognize when it's the Holy Spirit guiding you and when it's not?
- How do you communicate with others that the Holy Spirit is guiding you?
- Can you identify a recent example of when the Holy Spirit guided you?

Lesson 9

Seek Lasting Peace

In 2015, at the peak of Greece receiving almost nine hundred thousand refugees fleeing from Turkey and Syria, A21 had the privilege of working alongside a number of partner organizations, including the United Nations Refugee Agency (UNHCR).[1] The UNHCR was established in 1950 in the aftermath of the Second World War to help the millions of people who had lost their homes. Today their mission is much the same, as they work in 137 countries providing life-saving assistance, including shelter, food, water, and medical care for people forced to flee conflict and persecution.[2]

When our team worked alongside them in the refugee camps, members of the United Nations teams were easily identifiable by the blue helmets they wore. If you've ever watched news coverage of disasters around the world, or post-wartime efforts where injured people need to be rescued, then you may have seen them as they are often the first to rush in and carry the wounded to safety. They are known for heroically running in even when it means putting their own lives at risk.

Famously depicted on their blue helmets is the same image found on the UN flag—a map of the world inside a globe with an olive branch on either side. This reflects their global peacekeeping mission, as the olive branch is known for being a universal sign of peace.

I love the imagery of the olive branch, mostly because of where it first originated—in the Bible! That's right. It all began in Genesis 5, when a man named Noah was called by God to do something that had never been done before—to build an ark. Noah obeyed God and spent approximately 120 years building the ark to protect himself, his family, and seven pairs of clean animals and a pair of every other animal—all because God told him that he was going to bring rain and flood the earth.[3]

Do you remember this story? Once they boarded, they were stuck in the ark for more than a year because God flooded the earth, and even when the rain stopped after forty days and forty nights, they had to wait for the water to recede—and it receded *slowly* the Word says.[4] Can you imagine listening to the sound of rain for days on end when you'd never heard or felt rain? I love Nick and our girls and even our dog, Ezra. But I would have most certainly gotten cabin fever, and the germaphobe in me would have struggled, to say the least.

It had to be smelly. There had to be rough seas. The wind would have howled. Maybe they had bouts of seasickness. Maybe there were cases of claustrophobia. Did they have lamps or were they in total darkness much of the time? It's possible you've never wondered about any of this, but this is how my mind works. How did they wash their clothes or prepare their meals? What did they eat? Where did they go to the bathroom? What did they do to entertain themselves? What did they talk about? I have so many more questions for Noah—and his wife and family—but I'll save them for when I get to meet him in eternity someday.

Meanwhile, what we do know from Genesis 8 is that "God remembered Noah, as well as all the wildlife and all the livestock that were with him in the ark. God caused a wind to pass over the earth, and the water began to subside. . . . The water steadily receded from the earth, and by the end of 150 days the water had decreased significantly."[5]

Eventually enough water receded that the tops of the mountains became visible. Forty days after that, Noah first tested if the land was dry by sending out a raven, but the raven could only fly back and forth with nowhere to land.[6] Next he sent out a dove, but "the dove found no resting place for its foot. It returned to him in the ark because water covered the surface of the whole earth. He reached out and brought it into the ark to himself."[7]

Noah then waited seven more days and sent out another dove from the ark. This time things went much better. "When the dove came to him at evening, there was a plucked olive leaf in its beak. So Noah knew that the water on the earth's surface had gone down."[8]

This is where the symbolism of the olive branch representing peace first began. The olive leaf (or branch) was a sign for Noah that it was nearing the time to disembark. It served as proof that the floodwaters had receded enough that an olive tree was growing. It was a sign that God was working, and his purposes would come to pass. God had not forgotten that he promised to make a covenant with Noah that is evident to this day—God has never flooded the earth again, and we have the rainbow as a reminder. The olive branch was a sign of so much hope—that the flood was over, mankind was at peace with God, and it was time for a fresh start.

Where We Find True Peace

Sometimes it seems like the days in which we live are somewhat like the days Noah lived in because they are full of chaos. I think we'd all agree we live in a world full of anger, injustice, pain, suffering, arguing, violence, hatred, and opposing views, where people feel so passionate about their perspectives that it leads to chaos—sometimes to the point of killing one another. We need only to scroll through the news on our phones to see evidence of this around the globe—from reports on active shooters to invasions, to wars, riots, and genocides, to seeing thousands of displaced people vulnerable to starvation, disease, and human trafficking. There are constant speculations about peace talks in one country or another, and sometimes peace is successfully brokered, but even then, ultimately, it never seems to bring lasting peace.

There are times when it seems as though the whole world is walking around on eggshells, and some days we are much the same. Though we may start our day determined to keep our peace, something invariably happens, and we totally lose it. A car pulls out in front of us without warning, and a low level of road rage kicks in. One of our kids forgets to tell us we needed to pick them up after school, and we have to scramble to shift our schedule. The doctor's office calls with concerning news about a biopsy, and our heart starts to race. Our workplace begins a layoff, and we lose sleep. We think a relationship we've invested time and energy into is destined for marriage, but it begins to deteriorate instead, and a knot grows in our stomach. We don't get accepted at our first choice for college, and we start to doubt our worth and value. A friend doesn't return a text message, and our mind starts thinking of worst-case scenarios (yes, it can be something as simple as that).

I've watched as our girls and their friends have grown up with smartphones in their hands—something neither Nick nor I nor any parents in our generation ever had to deal with. If I wanted to call my mum and tell her I was leaving one friend's house to go to another friend's house, I had to use a phone attached to the wall that was connected to a landline. (If you are too young to know what I'm talking about, then google it.)

The point is that with the convenience of our smartphones has come plenty of ways to lose our peace. In fact, people who fall into the generations we call millennials and Gen Z are considered the most anxious generation.[9] This is based on multiple reasons, including managing student loan debt with the worry about their own futures and getting the best jobs, but one contributing factor in particular is the immediate access we all have on our phones to everything happening in this world.[10] None of us are capable of reading about one catastrophe after another and keeping our peace. Bingeing on social media or news content about troubling events is called *doomscrolling* or *doomsurfing*, and it can take a toll on our mental health.[11] It can cause feelings of uncertainty, anxiousness, worry, depression, fatigue, or psychological distress. And such feelings can disrupt our "sleep, appetite, motivation, or desire to do the things [we] often enjoy."[12]

Another reason this generation is so anxious is the pressure to manage the effects of social media—from dealing with curating the perfect presence on our newsfeed, to FOMO, to the chronic comparison of our lives with other people's lives, to the pressure for immediate results about most anything.[13] And truth be told, this particular issue isn't just a problem for the younger generations; we're all faced with it. Sometimes it's better for our peace of mind to take time off social media, to put our phones away during meals, and set any other boundaries we need.

It's shocking how easily we can lose our peace, even when our intentions are to keep it. What's worse is how exhausting it is to live on the verge of such internal chaos from one moment to the next. It is little wonder the word *peace* is mentioned as many as 429 times in the Bible[14] and that Jesus, who Isaiah calls the Prince of Peace, came to earth to give us his peace.[15] He knew we would need it. Left to our own devices, we are more likely to look for peace in places where we will never find it.

Sure, binge-watching a series on our favorite device, scrolling through our phones for hours on end, or overeating, drinking, partying, shopping, or medicating can provide temporary relief. But that underlying sense of agitation will still be there when reality sets in again. Ultimately, there's only one kind of peace that lasts—and it's the peace that Jesus gives, the peace that defies all logic, the peace he promised us before he left this earth. "Peace I leave with you. My peace I give to you. I do not give to you as the world gives. Don't let your heart be troubled or fearful."[16]

The Power of Peace

Because I come from a background of profound trauma, in my growing-up years I did not often experience peace of any kind in my home or my heart. It was not until I became a follower of Jesus that I found peace, even though for a long time thereafter many of my external circumstances did not change. I had to learn how to have peace in the midst of chaos. My family didn't agree with the direction of my newfound faith, which caused a lot of tension and heated debates at home. All my relatives—and there were lots of them—openly expressed what I could do differently to attract a husband, as they were never happy about my marital status all the years that I was single. Nor did any of them approve of my leaving a corporate job to work in the nonprofit sector. And when I went to work in the Christian nonprofit world, well, that was really a tipping point for all their angst. It was in those days that I learned to stay rooted in Christ. Philippians 4:6–7 became a lifeline for me—something I still cling to for peace of mind: "Don't worry about anything, but in everything, through prayer and petition with thanksgiving, present your requests to God. And the peace of God, which surpasses all understanding, will guard your hearts and minds in Christ Jesus."

At that time, there was little I could do to change my physical circumstances, but prayer was the portal through which I could access the supernatural peace of God in the midst of the chaos. I am grateful that I learned this early in my Christian walk, because since then my life and ministry have only become more complicated, not less, as God has entrusted me—and Nick— with the stewardship of so many more initiatives. To this very moment I have to choose to bring my requests to God through prayer and petition with thanksgiving every single day if I want to walk in supernatural peace.

The Hebrew word most commonly used in the Old Testament for *peace* is *shalom*. The fullness of its meaning includes "rightness, wholeness, that comes first and foremost from a right relationship with God."[17] Out of that right relationship with God, *shalom* refers to living with a sense of restfulness, contentment, and beauty—of living in harmony with God and with others.[18]

Truth be told, *shalom* sounds . . . otherworldly, doesn't it? How far are we from that description? More than millions of light-years away! But things weren't always the way they are today! Before sin entered the world in Genesis 3, all of God's creation experienced *shalom*, as all was good and as God intended it to be. In this world, *shalom* was a reality. But once Adam and Eve chose to sin, *shalom* ceased to be. In place of righteousness and rightness, there was and is sin. In place of wholeness, there was and is brokenness. In place of relationship, there was and is division. And that is the extremely short list of sin's consequences.

All of us are well aware of the effects of sin, both ours and that of others. We experience pain. We experience sorrow. We experience grief. We experience loss. We experience betrayal. And on the list goes. And living in a world marred and marked by sin, what is often our reality? Not *shalom* but pseudo-peace, not peace from within but peace that is contingent on our circumstances.

How long does pseudo-peace last? Only as long as our circumstances are good, easy, and ideal. When our health is strong, we're at peace. When our children and family members are healthy and well, we're at peace. When we get to laugh and joke and enjoy dinner with friends, we're at peace. When we participate in our interests and hobbies or volunteer at our church or in our communities, we're at peace. When we get to get out and be in nature doing what we love—we're at peace. When our work is secure and fulfilling, we're at peace. When our dreams and goals begin to flourish, we're at peace. But when these things change, so does our so-called peace, and we find ourselves tossed about perpetually in a sea of anxiety.

This is not the life that God intends for us; there is better!

While it's true that absolute *shalom*—meaning all things set right as God intends—won't occur until Jesus returns and establishes the new heaven and new earth, that doesn't mean we can't experience God's enduring, unshakable peace here and now. Peace is something God wants us to walk in regardless of our circumstances, including all the times that our relationships and everyday events challenge it and begin to rob us of it.

> Peace is something God wants us to walk in regardless of our circumstances.

In the New Testament, the word for *peace* is the Greek word *eiréné*.[19] Yes, it's the same name the Greeks gave to the goddess who held up an olive branch. It also happens to be a word I heard my Greek mother use multiple times a day when my brothers and I would chase one another through the house, tease one another unmercifully, or yell at the top of our lungs, "Tag, you're it!" All she wanted was some *eiréné*, which was almost impossible in a Greek house full of Greek drama.

Biblically, *eiréné* expresses a tranquility in our soul that isn't affected by outward circumstances or pressures. It's an inner stability that's not easily upset.[20] This is the peace we're truly after in our everyday affairs; this is the peace of mind we crave no matter what's happening around us or in the world. And when we get right down to it, there's only one place we'll ever consistently find this peace—in Jesus. It's what we receive when we receive Jesus. Therefore, it is not dependent upon our external circumstances but flows from the inside out when we depend on him. It is our reward for keeping ourselves rooted in Christ and pursuing steady growth. When we allow God to do a deep work in us, it shows in the fruit of our lives—which includes the fruit of peace.[21]

Never have I seen such peace exemplified more powerfully than when I was at a meeting in Southeast Asia with five hundred leaders from the underground church in a country where Christians are being persecuted. Many of them had been ostracized because of their faith, some to the point of losing their jobs and everything they owned. What's more astounding is that every single one of them had been imprisoned because of their faith at some point in their lives. They lived daily with the reality of being taken from their families and imprisoned again—or worse—and yet they exhibited a supernatural peace that defied understanding.

And they are not the only ones. Over the course of my ministry life, I've had the opportunity to visit many such followers of Jesus in a number of countries where Christians have experienced persecution for their faith. Their stories are similar. They are fully aware that they might die for their faith, but they have no fear—that is having the peace that surpasses all understanding. That is having the peace of God internally, so they can walk in the peace of God externally. That is having the peace of God that he makes available for each and every one of us.

Even as I'm writing this, yet another war has broken out, global warming is growing worse, and here in the States we're about to enter another chaotic election cycle. And independent of what is going on in the world, I know you have your own challenges and so do I. Yet in the midst of the changing circumstances, we have a promise. Jesus, who is the same yesterday, today, and forever, is the Prince of Peace who gives us perfect peace because he gives us himself. May we be those who hold fast to him and his every promise, letting the peace of Christ rule our hearts![22]

LESSONS LEARNED

- The olive branch is a symbol of peace.
- Jesus is the true peace we're to have internally, particularly in a world where there is no peace externally.
- Peace is something we have to learn to walk in every day.

QUESTIONS FOR REFLECTION

- Have you experienced peace with God so you can have the peace of God (Romans 5:1)?
- Can you identify things in your life right now that might be trying to steal your peace?
- What steps can you take to let peace rule your heart and fill your mind instead?

Lesson 10

Extend an Olive Branch

S ophia!"
Catherine yelled only one word, but it told me volumes. I was downstairs; Catherine and Sophia were upstairs. I was leaning against the kitchen island and having my morning coffee; they were upstairs about to have war, and most certainly over makeup. Listening to the next bits and pieces that ensued, I continued holding out hope that I would get five minutes of solitude and silence before I might have to intervene and begin hostage negotiations over the eyeliner . . . yet again. Clearly, I must have been delirious to hope for such things with an eighteen-year-old and twenty-two-year-old sharing a bathroom with makeup strewn across the counter—particularly since I thought we'd bought an ample supply so there would be no more fights over such a small thing. And yet, I'll admit, it's usually the small things that become the big things we all fight over. Alas, here we were again.

"You always take my stuff. You have a job, so you can buy your own," I heard Catherine plead.

Obviously, the latest round of peace talks and cease-fire

agreements weren't working. All I could do was take a deep breath, try to leave the tension where it needed to stay—between them—and take another sip of coffee. If you have girls or, better yet, had sisters, then you know all about this. I knew they'd work it out, but seriously, I could have closed my eyes and seen them as four and eight years old all over again. Hearing them fight over makeup wasn't much different than when I'd listen to them squabble over a toy or who got to go first. Now it was all about makeup, clothes, shoes—oh, and purses. When one of them borrowed a purse and forgot to ask permission from its rightful owner, it was always best that I go for a run, a walk, or a bike ride—whatever got me out of earshot and out of the line of fire.

"Mom," Sophia began as she descended the stairs.

"Stop right there," I interrupted her. "I heard it all. Go back upstairs and extend an olive branch to your sister. Make things right before you leave for work."

I wasn't completely unwilling to hear Sophia out, but this tug-of-war over makeup had been going on for a while. From my perspective, the heart of the issue was more about how they were treating each other than the unwelcome sharing of cosmetics. So when I told her to go extend an olive branch, she knew exactly what I meant: to go make peace with her sister.

Be a Peacemaker

I imagine one of the hardest things for any of us to do is extend an olive branch. It's not easy to be the first one to say, "I'm wrong," or "I'm sorry," or "Please forgive me." It's not easy being the first one to overlook an offense, the first one to go out of our way to not keep a false sense of peace and instead truly seek peace.

But as difficult as it may be, it's what God wants us to do; it's part of the fruit we're called to bear in this life.[1] Jesus told us in Matthew 5:9, "Blessed are the peacemakers, for they will be called sons of God." Notice that Jesus did not say blessed are the peacekeepers or peace avoiders. He did not say, "Blessed are the peace wishers or the peace hopers or the peace dreamers or the peace lovers or the peace talkers."[2] No. He said, "Blessed are the peacemakers."

To be a peacemaker means to be someone "who is actively seeking to reconcile people to God and to one another." In fact, "the word *make* in the term *peacemakers* comes from the Greek verb that means 'to do,' and it's a word bursting with energy."[3]

This shows us two things: First, being a peacemaker is not a passive behavior based on someone's personality or easy-going temperament. It's not based on someone's Enneagram number, even if they are a nine and identified as "the peacemaker."[4] Instead, it's solely based on being more of who we are in Christ. Being a peacemaker reflects our identity and character as children of God. And when we extend an olive branch to someone to proactively make peace, there's a blessing that comes. Remember, Jesus said, "Blessed are the peacemakers."

> Being a peacemaker reflects our identity and character as children of God.

Second, because we're children of God, we've been reconciled to God and then called to an actual ministry of reconciliation. It's out of this God-given ministry that we actively seek to reconcile people to God and to one another. Paul wrote that "everything is from God, who has reconciled us to himself through Christ and has given us the ministry of reconciliation. That is, in Christ, God was reconciling the world to himself, not counting their trespasses against them, and he has committed the message of reconciliation to us."[5]

What love God has for us that he entrusted to us the message of reconciliation! He trusts us to go about doing all we can to make peace, to bring reconciliation into every relationship where we have influence—particularly when we're personally challenged to be the first to say, "I'm sorry. I was wrong. Please forgive me."

To make this even more clear for us, let me share a little bit of Greek with you, because you know, I'm little and I'm Greek and I can't help myself! The Greek word used for *reconciled* is *diallassomai*, which refers to "mutual concession after mutual hostility." The idea of concession is "giving up an argument, surrendering a point, conceding to someone else, or letting something go and refusing to let it be an issue."[6]

When I sent Sophia back up the stairs to extend an olive branch to Catherine, this is what she did. She conceded her position, and when I heard what came next, I was so grateful that she got the bigger picture so quickly. She was remorseful, starting her apology with, "I'm sorry" and "I was wrong." She acknowledged that fighting over eyeliner wasn't worth what it did to the two of them and their mornings. She was in a hurry to get to work, so they didn't go on to figure out a solution, but they were well on their way. They at least agreed to be right with each other, and that was the most important point, especially for my heart.

What gives me the most hope is that if they can learn to do this over eyeliner, then they can learn to do it over the bigger things to come in life—because the bigger things will come. In our humanity, in all our relationships, there will be misunderstandings, confusion, assumptions, and misperceptions. There will be disappointments, disagreements, and hurt feelings with one another. And the temptation to be offended will rise up. The question we'll always face in those moments is, "What will we do with it all?"

If we've taken the time to root ourselves deep in God; if we've taken the time to pursue slow, steady growth; if we're continuing to grow in resiliency; and we're being fruitful; then reconciliation will be part of how we walk.

Reconciliation is a process that requires acknowledging, repenting, righting the wrong if we've left another at a disadvantage, rebuilding trust, and—where possible—restoring.[7] Why are each of these elements so essential? Without acknowledgment, there is no confidence the wrong is seen or understood as wrong and no assurance that it won't be repeated. Without repentance—a ceasing and returning from the wrong—there is continual damage to the relationship. Without trust there can't be a healthy relationship. Simply said, there have to be actions that speak louder than words.

As hard as it may seem, as Jesus followers we've been called to be at peace with others, to help others be reconciled to God, and to do all we can to help others be at peace with one another. It sounds like a full-time job, doesn't it? It sounds like a lot of hard work. No wonder most of us get so overwhelmed, have no idea where to start, and would rather just watch another rerun of The Crown. But if you are anything like me, then you can only ignore the prompting of the Holy Spirit for so long before you have to begin the process of making things right with someone—as far as it is in your power to do so. Paul said as much when he wrote to the Romans: "If possible, as far as it depends on you, live at peace with everyone."[8]

No doubt we all have situations where we know we need to extend an olive branch. Taking the first step can be daunting and even a bit messy, but remember: It's something God wants us to do, though we are only responsible for so much ("as far as it depends on you").

Knowing what I'm responsible for and what I'm not responsible for helps me not only take the first step but trust God as I prepare to take that first step, whether it's a phone call or an in-person conversation. I've also put into play some spiritual practices to get internal peace before I try to make external peace, starting with prayer. I spend time talking to God about the situation. I position my heart to receive what he might show me— first and foremost about myself, then about the other person, and finally about how to begin a conversation that's constructive. I often remind myself that peace has to begin with me. If I go to someone all stirred up emotionally, ready to defend myself, the reconciliation I hope for probably won't happen. I'll be in my own way, and that's not what any of us want.

When I sense that the timing is right and the other person has agreed, I go and have the conversation I've been praying about and preparing for so earnestly. When I speak, I tell the truth in love and stick to the facts. This helps me stay on point and keep the issue the issue rather than letting my feelings muddy the situation. I do my best to display the fruit of the Spirit, namely gentleness and patience, and when I do, people tend to be far more receptive to what I have to say. When I am patient, it gives me the endurance I need to work through things, especially when the process takes more time than I expect. Not every reconciliation happens in one meeting. Sometimes it takes coming together multiple times to reach a place of understanding, accepting, or agreeing to disagree.

I've also learned the importance of talking only to the person with whom there's an offense and not venting to anyone else. If we share with others, it can quickly turn into gossip and harm even more people. Next, I get myself in the frame of mind to be willing to listen. To lean back. To have a mental and physical posture that is poised to deescalate the situation and not incite any further misunderstandings. James reminded us, "Everyone should be quick to listen, slow to speak, and slow to anger, for human anger does not accomplish God's righteousness."[9]

God wants us to be peacemakers who make peace, who make the effort to reconcile with others. Our differences are meant to be resolved if at all possible, and that takes someone—like you and me—extending an olive branch to hopefully bring it all about. Granted, the reality is that not everyone we go to will want to be reconciled. That's where the "if possible, as far as it depends on you" part comes into play.

> God wants us to be peacemakers who make peace, who make the effort to reconcile with others.

Furthermore, I can't close out this section without saying that in some situations forgiveness will be necessary but reconciliation will be impossible or unwise. In my own journey of forgiving the men who abused me as a child, I had to learn the difference between forgiveness and reconciliation. I read the words of Jesus: "For if you forgive others their offenses, your heavenly Father will forgive you as well. But if you don't forgive others, your Father will not forgive your offenses."[10] I knew I had to forgive. After all, I wanted my offenses forgiven, and I wanted to be free from the prison of unforgiveness and bitterness. But I certainly did not feel safe around those men. And years later, because they were still around my extended family, I did not want my children to be anywhere near them—and that is exactly how I should have felt because they were not safe people.

I don't want you to think that forgiveness requires putting yourself in any kind of physical, emotional, or spiritual danger, because it does not. If there has been a history of violence or physical, mental, emotional, or spiritual abuse or other danger-ous practices, it's clearly not safe to reconcile. I'm highlighting this because I'm aware that much damage can be caused by confusing forgiveness—which Jesus commanded—with recon-ciliation, which is the goal when a relationship can and should be restored. Some people are not safe because they are unwilling to do the work to become healed and whole. Therefore, it's wise to create boundaries to ensure your safety and, in some circum-stances, the safety of your loved ones.

When Someone Else Doesn't Want Peace

Having clarified some very important things to take into consid-eration when seeking reconciliation, I do want to emphasize that clearly, Jesus gave us the responsibility for reconciliation where it is possible. Jesus took this call to reconciliation seriously enough to mention it in the Sermon on the Mount, the same message where he said, "Blessed are the peacemakers." He said, "So if you are offering your gift on the altar, and there you remember that your brother or sister has something against you, leave your gift there in front of the altar. First go and be reconciled with your brother or sister, and then come and offer your gift."[11]

Can you imagine being in church, all poised to worship and give God your all, when you suddenly realize that you need to get up and go be reconciled with someone first? I'm not sure I've ever turned to Nick and said, "I'll be right back. Hold on to my gift. I've got to go make something right first," but I'd like to think I'd be willing to.

Jesus said that if we discover that we have something against someone or that someone has something against us, no matter the size of the issue, we should address it *first*. It could be something we said in passing or was said to us. It could be something intended as harmless, to the point we are tempted to dismiss it. But from what Jesus said, even the little things that have become a barrier need to be settled. After all, it's mostly the little things that aggravate us, and when left unaddressed, those little bricks of offense become great walls.

It's so easy to gloss over offense and muffle what the Holy Spirit is showing us, but when we feel hurt, angst, bitterness, anger, or resentment, then we need to get to the bottom of it. Sometimes there will be infractions or offenses that are small enough and out of character for the other person that we can forgive them and "overlook an offense." For example, if we know a person is having a bad day, we are able to forgive them and move on with a clean heart toward them. This is very different from when we put on our "public face," step out of the house, and pretend everything is all right, but in private we let down the facade and ruminate over what someone did to us and why we're justified in not reaching out first. When that happens, we definitely need to initiate reconciliation.

Who is it that you need to be reconciled to? What is it that you haven't wanted to face? That you haven't wanted to deal with? That you keep avoiding in hopes that the issue will get swept under the rug and never come out into the light? All in the hope that you won't have to humble yourself and face the humiliation and embarrassment that might ensue? All because your pride is standing in the way?

Ouch. I know. I felt that as I wrote it, but I say it to you because I'm saying it to myself. Even as I'm writing this book, I'm navigating a personal relationship where there was a misunderstanding, but the person seemingly doesn't want to have any further conversations to possibly work things out. I'm the kind of person who wants to talk it all out on the phone or meet face-to-face to clear the air. I want to clarify the events that happened and the words, sentences, and paragraphs that were said so I can gain understanding and so reconciliation is possible. But what do we do if the other person doesn't want to engage? What do we do in such a messy situation? Particularly when we've done all that the Bible tells us to do?

Extending an olive branch and trying to make peace is such a risk because not everyone will meet us halfway. As shocking as it sounds, not everyone will want to reconcile—even when they're a fellow Christ follower. Even if we once walked with them, learned from them, exchanged gifts, attended Bible study and raised our kids together, went through gut-wrenching times with them, and were the best of prayer partners.

In times like that, when you've done all that you know to do, when you've prayed and reached out with the purest of intentions, you have to give it all to God. You have to grieve the loss and invite Jesus in to heal your heart while leaving the branch extended and refusing to do anything that would make it less likely for them to take hold of the branch in the future.

As far as it depends on you, are you at peace with everyone? Is there a step you need to take today? If you sense you have something against someone, go to them. Today. If you sense they have something against you, go to them. Today. And as you extend the olive branch, trust in God's power and find peace in his promise: "Blessed are the peacemakers!"

LESSONS LEARNED

- God has called us to be peacemakers, to extend an olive branch whenever possible.
- A peacemaker is someone who is actively seeking to reconcile people to God and to one another.
- Because we're children of God, we have been reconciled to God, and then called to an actual ministry of reconciliation.

QUESTIONS FOR REFLECTION

- Understanding what a peacemaker is, have there been times in your life when you have been a peacekeeper rather than a peacemaker?
- Are you in the practice of offering olive branches when needed?
- Is there someone in your life now that you need to extend an olive branch to?

Lesson 11

Disturb the Peace

When I was first awakened to the horrors of human trafficking in Thessaloniki, Greece, and became convinced that I was to do something about it, I thought everyone would be as passionate as I was about eradicating this injustice. Surely, I reasoned, we all know that slavery is evil. Surely we all agree that children need to be protected from predators. Surely we who believe that every human being is created in the image of God and is worthy of value, dignity, esteem, and freedom should be at the forefront of advocating for victims and helping to eradicate any systems of injustice that enable human trafficking.

But as I began to speak out against this evil, the one thing I did not anticipate and was not ready for was the resistance I encountered. People of faith—and also those with no faith at all—felt that by raising awareness about human trafficking in Greece, I was trying to belittle and shame the nation's people and culture. Some pastors felt that church was not the place to talk about such things and that it would distract people from the gospel and Scripture. Yet it was no secret that Greece had a history with human trafficking, so why wouldn't everyone be on board with wanting to eradicate it? I had done my research, and it was well known that Greece was the parking lot of human trafficking in Europe.[1]

At the time we started the work of A21, Thessaloniki was the best European location to fight global slavery because it was in the middle of the biggest gateway that illegal migrants followed into Europe. Traffickers knew this route, as it had been used for thousands of years for slave trade. Even the apostle Paul encountered this heinous crime when he intersected with a slave girl on his way to a place of prayer in the city of Philippi, a mere two-hour car ride northeast of Thessaloniki.[2] Just as in biblical times, modern-day traffickers had been preying on innocent victims there for years—luring them from impoverished nations with promises of work and hope for a better life. And to this very day, Greece still serves as the backdoor entry point for close to 90 percent of illegal immigrants to the European Union. And yes, this number includes those transported illegally for purposes of sexual exploitation.[3]

The problem was that when I first began to speak out about the issue, few people wanted to face the reality that such a crime existed in their nation and that something needed to be done about it. It took several years of raising awareness about trafficking before the tide began to turn. Today, thankfully, organizations across Greece—along with individuals and churches around the world—partner with A21 in a variety of ways. I'm grateful that so many churches and Christians now see this as part of our responsibility to fight injustice wherever we see it and recognize it's something Jesus did when he walked the earth.

The same man who said, "Blessed are the peacemakers," and taught us about forgiveness and extending olive branches not only went about doing good, healing the oppressed, and delivering and raising the dead but also stood up against injustice.[4] In fact, in his very first recorded sermon delivered in the synagogue, Jesus proclaimed, "The Spirit of the Lord is on me, because he has anointed me to preach good news to the poor. He has sent me to proclaim release to the captives and recovery of sight to the blind, to set free the oppressed, to proclaim the year of the Lord's favor."[5] Did you catch that? Jesus himself said that there was a reason the Spirit of the Lord was upon him.

The Gospels are full of accounts of Jesus reaching out to the poor, the ostracized, the marginalized, the oppressed, and the disenfranchised—and then giving them value, dignity, esteem, and freedom. One of those incidents that has always deeply impacted me is when Jesus entered the temple in Jerusalem during Passover and began flipping over the tables of the money changers and the merchants who were selling animals. The account is in Matthew's gospel: "Jesus went into the temple and threw out all those buying and selling. He overturned the tables of the money changers and the chairs of those selling doves. He said to them, 'It is written, my house will be called a house of prayer, but you are making it a den of thieves!'"[6]

Now, you might be thinking that this is somewhat of an overreaction from Jesus and wondering what this has to do with taking a stand against injustice and oppression, but knowing a little more about the historical and cultural context helps to make that clear. You see, in those days, people from all over Israel had to come to Jerusalem to celebrate Passover and offer their sacrifices in the temple. Knowing that, people set up shop within the temple and sought to capitalize off those coming to worship God. It was completely acceptable to purchase cattle, sheep, or doves outside the temple to sacrifice them inside. But it was not acceptable that the money changers—the people who exchanged Roman coins considered pagan for kosher sheqels[7]— and the merchants selling the animals made a profit that took unfair advantage of the people. Commerce for profit was taking place in a sacred space and the devout were being cheated, particularly the vulnerable out-of-towners and the poor.[8] That's what Jesus was referring to when he said, "but you are making it a den of thieves!"

Because of this context, I don't see this as an overreaction from Jesus but rather a disturbing of the pseudo-peace in order to get real peace. I see a disrupting of the status quo to show that injustice and oppression were taking place. When we read carefully through the Gospels, it is evident that Jesus did not spend his entire ministry life flipping tables. But when he did, he did it for a purpose; he did it to confront an injustice, to right a wrong. What's more, he has called us to do the same. It's part of our fruitfulness.

Ways We Make Peace

Our advocacy, through the work of A21 and on behalf of the vulnerable and the marginalized who are being exploited, could be seen as a modern-day form of flipping tables. Our team sees the men, women, and children who are being exploited for forced labor, domestic servitude, and sex work, and we can't look away. We have accepted the call of God to be peacemakers in this world, to bear his fruit, but like Jesus demonstrated, we also have learned that sometimes you have to disturb the peace in order to make peace. If we're going to stop human trafficking, then we're going to have to disturb the peace of anyone who's complacent, ignorant, or indifferent toward this issue. We're going to have to disturb the peace of any country, government, or law enforcement agency that's grown tolerant of such crimes and is willing to put up with the status quo.

Just recently we saw fifty-two young women identified and assisted out of sex trafficking in Greece and twenty traffickers captured in one raid. When I shared this with a friend who knows me all too well, she said, "Chris, you had to flip some tables and disturb the status quo to wake people up to the reality of human trafficking in our country, but look at what the Lord has done."

I'm not at all suggesting that we make a ministry or a calling or a passion out of flipping tables wherever we go. We're not called to disturb the peace without a valid cause in society at large, in our communities, in our workplaces, in our families, or anywhere else we have influence. But when we become aware of an injustice, we most certainly are called to stand up for what is right. Moreover, we have a responsibility to examine our hearts to ensure that our motives are pure and not possibly misguided by our anger, false information, or someone else's frenzy.

> When we become aware of an injustice, we most certainly are called to stand up for what is right.

Every time I start to disturb the peace, in any given situation, I ask myself, *Why am I doing this? Is this a personal agenda? Or is this something the Lord is asking me to do?* Because none of us can speak up about everything all the time. In fact, Ecclesiastes 3:7 tells us that there is a time to speak and a time to be silent. There are a thousand issues I could be speaking about everywhere God sends me, but I can't speak on every issue. I can only speak about the issues God shows me, much like he did when he put missing women and children on my heart in the Thessaloniki airport so many years ago. We have to keep in mind that when Jesus flipped the tables outside the temple, his motives were pure because he couldn't sin. But for us, we're more than capable of sin, so we have to check ourselves.

I also point this out because we live in the age of social media, where there's a public platform for anyone to vent and lash out about anything—to flippantly flip a table—without accountability, without accurate information, and without any responsibility for how many people we can possibly hurt. It's so easy to unknowingly get caught up in the anger and divisiveness that permeates our world today and start flipping tables online without doing anything to solve the issue in real life offline.

We can so often feel justified and self-righteous as we call things out, join in on arguments on social media, and get involved in the cancel culture of our day—something indicative of a behavior *Psychology Today* says has grown into a phenomenon known as *emotional contagion*.[9] The name alone sounds like something none of us want, but if we've been emotionally influenced by a post to the point we've commented on it and joined an ongoing disagreement—often without knowing all the facts or with a limited understanding of the issue's complexities—then we've been infected. What's more, without face-to-face interaction, there isn't a way to recognize the hurt we have the power to inflict. By adding to the noise, standing up for what we think is injustice often creates more injustice. We have to keep in mind that the purpose is always to make peace, not stir up more strife, division, and hurt.

We need to be wise about when and how to flip tables. After all, we only see one example of Jesus using this method of peacemaking in Scripture. What's more, I think we are all aware that any change we want to see happen in this world typically begins with us and in our own hearts and lives. Whether it's changing a habit, improving our relationships, or course correcting the direction we're headed, it begins with flipping a table in our own hearts and minds; it begins with confronting ourselves first and foremost. More than once, when I've been desperate for change and have prayed to God for him to move in a situation—namely by moving in someone else's heart—in his great mercy he has shown me what I needed to do first. It involved me, not them. He has shown me how my perspective needed to shift first, how my behavior or my words needed to be adjusted first, how I needed to ask for forgiveness first.

It's so natural in our eagerness to see change to want everyone else to change first, but God often starts with us, doesn't he? And if we don't stay sensitive to the conviction of the Holy Spirit in our own lives, then he'll help us by sending someone to point out what we can't see. Teaching as often as I do, I do my best to speak the truth in love. But I'm fully aware that I have to be equally willing to receive the truth when it's spoken in love to me.[10] And to be honest, like most of us, I don't particularly like it when I'm on the receiving end. When you communicate as much as I do, in a sense you get used to telling people how they should live. So when someone tells me how I should change, or when I've said or done something wrong, it sometimes takes me a hot minute to appreciate the truth they're speaking. I suppose I find myself in that place most often with Nick, as he knows me best and is faithful to tell me when I didn't get it right, or say it right, or need to go make it right. When he decides to confront me, I'll admit that in that moment I don't always think about how he's loving me and helping me. Rather, I suddenly discover a hundred truths I'd love to speak to him "in love," but that's not really how it's supposed to work, is it?

Having people in my life who are willing to disturb my peace to bring about real peace is a safeguard. It's kept me running my race all these years even though I have been far from perfect. I mean, you cannot be in ministry for as many decades as I have without having said things you wish you had said differently, or not at all, or without having done things that have at times hurt people, even if unintentionally. I have to continuously grow in Christlikeness just like every other Jesus follower. I, too, must be open, humble, and willing to be corrected and to change when necessary. The truth is, if we're the ones always flipping the tables and doing the confronting, there's something really wrong.

Peaceful Protests

When God put it on my heart to start the work of A21, I had to disturb the peace in my own life to do it. I had just turned forty and had my second baby girl, Sophia. I was traveling to churches and conferences and speaking about the good news of Jesus all over the world. I truly was not looking for something new to do. I didn't particularly want something new to do. Nick and I were happy with our marriage, our family life, and our ministry life.

But God disturbed my peace to bring about peace in the lives of the victims of human trafficking around the globe. And Nick agreed we were supposed to play a part in helping to stop this evil. He was willing to have our lives disrupted for all that God wanted to do. I remember discussing what such a move would do to our lives: We'd have to live traveling, almost nonstop. We'd be away from our families and friends in Australia much of the time. We'd have to raise our girls while taking them with us on the road. Everything about our homelife would look much different than we had planned. We had to be willing to have our own peace disturbed before we could start disturbing the peace that allowed human trafficking to take place. Still, we were all in.

For almost twenty years we have been metaphorically "flipping tables" through our prevention and awareness campaigns at A21. One of the most effective peaceful, nonviolent, "table flipping" campaigns we host in cities around the globe is our annual Walk for Freedom. Over the past decade we have hosted as many as five hundred walks on a single day in eighty countries. We've walked alongside hundreds of thousands of participants who walk silently in single file while carrying signs to bring attention to all the men, women, and children who are trapped in slavery and whose voices have been silenced.

Another example is our Can You See Me? campaign. It's a global campaign with an antitrafficking awareness message seen on kiosks in airports, as banners on the sides of buses, and on billboards along interstate highways. It includes commercials and short films shown on television, in arenas before sports games, in hospitals, shopping malls, corporate offices, spas, restaurants, airports, and on planes. There are printed materials that target the most vulnerable in hot spots around the world, where people are being displaced due to war or natural disasters, often landing in refugee camps. You could say we're disturbing the peace of someone wanting to catch a bus or watch a movie on an airplane in order to once again make peace in the lives of millions caught in modern-day slavery—and our efforts have resulted in the recovery of countless people.

The call to disturb pseudo-peace in order to bring real peace is not just a call for me, and it's not just a call for the A21 team; it's a call for all of us as Christians. We are all called to be peacemakers as we seek for God's kingdom to come and for his will to be done here as it is in heaven. It's more of the fruitfulness God calls us to in our lives. What about you? Where is it that God is nudging you to disturb the peace, internally or externally, to make true peace?

> We are all called to be peacemakers as we seek for God's kingdom to come and for his will to be done here as it is in heaven.

Maybe you haven't been able to find the time to address what you need to do to take better care of yourself, most likely because you've been taking care of everyone else. It's time to disturb the peace to make real peace in your life and your health.

Maybe you've been avoiding a conversation that needs to take place—with a son or daughter, with another family member or friend—one that confronts the elephant in the room in order to move toward true healing and peace. It's time to disturb the peace to bring about real peace.

Maybe you've been dancing around a coworker, as has everyone else you work alongside, and it's time to be honest and loving and go to them in peace, to disturb the peace to make peace, for everyone's sake.

Maybe there is more God wants you to do in your church, in your community, or on behalf of the underserved and overlooked. Who is that? What is that? Now is the time to disturb your own peace, and perhaps that of others, to bring about real change and real peace.

Wherever it is that God is calling you to disturb the peace, prayerfully and bravely begin moving forward. I understand it won't be easy, but God will be with you, and he will bless you. After all, he promises us that the work of righteousness will be peace.[11]

LESSONS LEARNED

- Jesus stood up for injustice and so should we.
- Part of being a peacemaker is disturbing the peace.
- Sometimes you have to disturb the peace to attain true peace, first in our inner worlds and then in our external world where we see injustice.

QUESTIONS FOR REFLECTION

- Is there an area of your life—at home, work, church, community—where you know you need to disturb the peace to attain true peace? Is it something you've known but have been avoiding?
- Why is it that we might avoid disturbing the peace within ourselves first?
- What is your next step in disturbing the peace internally and externally?

Lesson 12

Produce Much Fruit

What I personally love most about olives, besides the taste, is that, surprisingly, they are actually a fruit—which characteristically means they come from a flower and they have a seed. I love to eat olives for breakfast, but not whole olives. I love what we Greeks call *epityrum*. It's essentially smashed-up olives, often mixed with other delightful ingredients like capers, sun-dried tomatoes, fresh basil, lemon juice, garlic, and the ever-essential extra-virgin olive oil.

Even though you're more likely to find olives with the vegetables in a supermarket, they belong to a family of fruit known as drupes, which are fruits that have one large stone, much like a peach, mango, or avocado.[1] And when an olive tree is flourishing, particularly if it is older and larger, it can produce as many as four hundred pounds of fruit annually.[2] That's roughly eighteen thousand olives a year. The point is that olive trees are extremely fruitful! No seed or crop produces as much return in one year as an olive does, because once you harvest an olive, you can press it up to four times and get not only olive oil but ingredients for cosmetics, medicine, and soaps. Even the pits can be crushed and used in energy production, as a thickening agent in cooking, and as a natural pesticide.[3]

Living olive trees produce fruit. That is what they do! Going back to David, who testified that he was like a flourishing olive tree in the house of God even in the midst of adversity, what do we see in his life? The same. Fruit. If we have eyes to see it. David was languishing. He was facing extreme hardship. He was facing tremendous opposition. Yet, in the midst of all that, he didn't become paralyzed. He didn't remain in that space mentally, emotionally, or spiritually. Instead, he stayed rooted, resilient, and fruitful. The grace of God was still flowing through his life to do the works—or produce the fruit—that God had for him. He was still flourishing and growing in his relationship with God. He was still being used by the Spirit of God to pen fresh songs of praise that are part of the Psalms today.

Clearly, producing fruit is not merely a subtheme in Scripture. In fact, the word *fruit* is used more than two hundred times, with more than sixty of those mentions being in the New Testament alone.[4] What's more, it's not something God is indifferent about. Toward the end of his earthly ministry, Jesus told his disciples, "My Father is glorified by this: that you produce much fruit, and prove to be My disciples."[5] The question for all of us is, how do we do that? Internally and externally?

His Fruit for His Glory

Worldwide, there are roughly 150 cultivars of olive trees producing the olives we enjoy.[6] And while the average size of an olive is one inch from top to bottom, olives are sorted into twelve categories based on size.[7] I won't go into them all, but suffice it to say that larger fruit are identified with names such as Atlas, Mammoth, and Colossal. And smaller fruit are identified with names like Superior, Brilliant, or Bullet.

Sizing up olives is helpful for harvesting and processing, but it's not an evaluation of the fruit's value. In the world of olives, every size is profitable. Every size is desirable. Every size serves a purpose. Furthermore, just because a tree produces large fruit does not mean it's more fruitful than a tree that produces small fruit. In fact, if you weighed the harvest of a tree bearing large fruit and that of a tree bearing small fruit and those yields weighed the same, the tree producing the small fruit would numerically have far more fruit. Depending on the size of the small olives, it might even have three times as much fruit.

With all this in mind, when it comes to our spiritual fruit, it's much the same idea. Just like no two varietals of olive trees produce the exact same size and yield of fruit, neither do we— because we're all so vastly different. We have all been made in the image of God, but we are so uniquely made.[8] That means that God has purposely created us to bear our own specific fruit—and the size, volume, and shape of that fruit will be different for each one of us.

At the same time, in a world full of comparison and competition where we're pressured to believe that bigger is better and more is better, it's so easy to fall into the trap of thinking that small fruit is insignificant or that not bearing as much fruit as someone else—in quantity or apparent impact—is a sign of failure. But that's not how God sees things, and that's not what he says.

Did God despise the widow's offering because the value of her mite was . . . so miniscule?[9] Did he see it as insignificant? Did he view her as a failure in who she was and in what she did and in what she had to offer? No, not at all. What about the man Jesus healed from demon possession? The man begged to go with Jesus and, surprisingly, Jesus would not permit him. Instead, Jesus told him, "Go home to your own people and report to them how much the Lord has done for you and how he has had mercy on you."[10]

Some people might look at that healed man's assignment in ministry as less significant because he wasn't traveling but the disciples were. He was more localized with less of a "reach." But was that seemingly smaller reach insignificant in God's eyes? No, and through the man's obedience, the gospel spread farther as it went beyond the Jewish borders and into the Greek world.

I am so grateful that God does not measure things like the world does. He makes it clear that he wants us to bear much fruit and be fruit that remains—and we each have our own fruit to bear. Just like one olive tree can't compare its fruit or yield to another, neither can we. All we're accountable for is producing the size and amount of fruit God created us to produce.

> The degree to which you are abiding in him is the degree to which you will experience fruitfulness in your life.

What's more, to produce the fruit that we're called to bear will require action on our part—but not the action of frenzied activity, rather the action of living our lives rooted and grounded in God.[11] In fact, the degree to which you are abiding in him is the degree to which you will experience fruitfulness in your life.

Just before Jesus said that it is to his Father's glory that we bear much fruit, he said this:

> Remain in me, and I in you. Just as a branch is unable to produce fruit by itself unless it remains on the vine, neither can you unless you remain in me. I am the vine; you are the branches. The one who remains in me and I in him produces much fruit, because you can do nothing without me.[12]

To remain is to abide in God's presence. It's to seek him with all our hearts and to cherish his words.[13] It's to believe what he says. It's to obey what he says. And it's to repent and ask forgiveness when we sin. Jesus went on to say, "If you remain in me and my words remain in you, ask whatever you want and it will be done for you."[14]

To remain is the "act of receiving and trusting all that God is for us in Christ."[15] Our relationship with God—and our fruitfulness—always goes back to trusting him, doesn't it? Even when we can't trace him. Even when we feel that we have reason to pause, to question, to cry out and lament.

To remain is to continually invite the Holy Spirit to fill us freshly, to transform us, to produce his good fruit in us.[16] In a world full of pain, suffering, chaos, arguing, strife, and division, we need a little more love, joy, peace, patience, kindness, goodness, faithfulness, gentleness, and self-control, don't we? Wouldn't our world be a very different place if the followers of Jesus released their fruit of the Spirit into the world?

I think one of the most effective witnessing tools in our generation could be the people of God reflecting the character of God in a world that lives so antithetically to the ways of

God. I love the fact that the fruit of the Spirit are not reserved for a special class of believers but are the fruit to be seen in every believer's life. And they make a difference in our homes, families, friendships, communities, workplaces, and world. And what a beautiful way to glorify God with our lives.

> One of the most effective witnessing tools in our generation could be the people of God reflecting the character of God in a world that lives so antithetically to the ways of God.

Whenever God's will and God's ways are being done in you and through your life as you rely on him, you are bearing fruit.

If you are honoring God's Word with faith and obedience, you're bearing fruit.

If you are seeking God's face and to know him more, you're bearing fruit.

If you're praying according to his will and in faith, you're bearing fruit.

If you're seeking and submitting to the Spirit's guidance, you're bearing fruit.

If you're growing in humility and crucifying pride, you're bearing fruit.

If you're turning from sin and pursuing holiness, you're bearing fruit.

If you're choosing forgiveness, you're bearing fruit.

If you're demonstrating the love of God as you serve and
   care for others, you're bearing fruit.

If you're putting God first and others ahead of yourself,
   you're bearing fruit.

If you're serving for the glory of God at home, at work, at
   school, at church, or anywhere, you're bearing fruit.

If you're acting in justice, mercy, and humility to align the
   world around you to his ways, you're bearing fruit.

If you're pursuing peace as much as it depends on you,
   you're bearing fruit.

If you're being patient and slow to anger, you're bearing fruit.

If you're sharing the love of Christ with a friend and have
   been for years, you're bearing fruit, even if they haven't
   come to Christ yet.

And it's worth saying: You don't have to see the fruit to trust
that God is producing fruit through you. Sometimes, fruit is
evident immediately. Sometimes it is evident eventually. Other
times it will be evident in eternity. Sometimes, when we are
planting the seed, we can't see the fruit. Other times, when we
are watering, we can sort of see it. But at all times, God is at work
and causing growth. We don't have confidence based on what we
see. We have confidence based on what he has said. If we remain
in him, we will bear much fruit for his glory!

God Watches Over the Seeds We Sow

Sophia has always loved books and has kept a journal from the
days she learned to write. And for this momma who has an

English literature degree, it has meant so much to me that we have spent her teenage years discussing the classics. The apple really does not fall far from the tree.

Watching her settle into college in Paris and this new time in her life makes me so happy for her, because this is her dream come true—though I'll admit it's not quite mine. I thought after launching Catherine off to college three years ago, I'd be fine with launching Sophia. But I wasn't quite ready for her to be 5,655 miles away, across an ocean and in another nation on a completely different continent. Especially since Catherine's university was only a two-hour drive from home.

I've decided there's nothing that elevates your prayer life quite like sending a kid off into the world to live on their own. As parents, we are well aware of all the possible pitfalls. We know the enemy is after our children and that he is a very real enemy. And we know that even if our children are responsible and dependable, they are still more vulnerable than they'll ever admit. The world can be a brutal place. What's more, we've all been their age. Let's just say my intercession in this season has gone to new levels.

Since Sophia has been away, I've wondered if all the seeds Nick and I have sown into her over the past eighteen years would bear fruit. All the late-night conversations, the answering of her million-plus questions, praying for her every day, taking her to church, prioritizing Bible reading, encouraging her gifts and talents, and having sometimes-heated discussions about friends and life choices. All of it. And then, out of nowhere Sophia FaceTimed me last week. I didn't have to call her first! And what she said left me utterly astounded at the goodness of God.

She wanted to tell me about an assignment for one of her

classes. Since 90 percent of the students at her university are from other countries, her professor assigned everyone to write about a piece of literature from their home country to share with the class so everyone could learn something about another nation.

What she said next caught me totally off guard. "Mom, I pondered this for a few days, and because I didn't know what to do, I emailed my professor. I told him that although I was born in Australia, I left Australia to move to America when I was four, so I don't really feel rooted in Australia as home. And even though I lived in America, my sister and I traveled to fifty countries during my middle school and high school years with our parents for their humanitarian work in establishing an organization to fight human trafficking. Because my mother is Greek, I do have a Greek passport, but I don't speak Greek, so I don't feel like Greece is my home country either.

"My idea for this assignment is the only thing that's been consistent throughout my eighteen years. No matter what continent or country we were in, it was the Christian Bible that felt most like home. So I asked him if it would be okay for me to write a paper on the literature of the Christian Bible, and he said yes. And then he said, 'That would be really interesting for you to write about the literature of the Bible.'"

Because she could see my face, and my reaction, you know what I did. I played it cool. I acted perfectly normal, like this was no big deal, like it was just another everyday occurrence. Because you know, if you act like something is a big deal with a teenager or young adult, well, it might go well for you, and it might not. So I responded with what I felt was the appropriate level of affirmation and enthusiasm. "That's great, Sophia. How innovative. Way to take the initiative. I'm so proud of you."

But when we ended our call, it was a whole different story. I burst out crying. I sobbed. To hear my child say that the only place that felt like home was the Bible wrecked me in the most beautiful way. I couldn't get over the fact that she's at an entirely secular college, in a profoundly secular nation, and her professor gave her the okay to write her assignment about the literature of the Bible. I was overcome at seeing just a glimpse of fruit from eighteen years of laboring as a parent, of all those years of answering her constant questions about God and faith and explaining what we were doing with our lives as a family and why we were prioritizing the purposes of God over everything else. How many times had I second-guessed myself and second-guessed how I'd answered her questions or explained why her dad and I believed like we did or felt like we felt. Parenting can be so exhausting in all the best possible ways, can't it?

When I finally pulled myself together, all I could do was thank God. I was so grateful for the seeds that had taken root in her heart and mind. And that God was so gracious to let me see it. Then, a little while later, it crossed my mind: *Do I believe that the Bible is my home?* To think that God used my own daughter to challenge me about where my home is.

I share all this well aware that Sophia is only just beginning her life. I know she's not perfect, that she's apt to make her own mistakes, that she's yet to fully mature and figure it all out. In fact, today is a new day, and I'm hoping she's doing really well—and I'll probably FaceTime her after I finish writing this lesson to be sure, but I'm not putting any pressure on her because of this glimpse. I'm just saying it is so reassuring when the Lord allows us to see some of the fruit of our labors.

To this day, I still pray over my girls that they'll be "like young olive trees around my table."[17] As grateful as I am for all the fruit that God has allowed me to bear around the world, nothing is more precious to me than my girls. And the thing I've prayed most is that my children would love Jesus, love his Word, love his people, and love a lost world.

I don't know what or who you hold most dear in this way. Maybe you've been interceding more than usual too. If you've done your best to give of your time, talent, treasure, heart, words, prayers, and actions, then trust God for the fruit. He is faithful to watch over our seeds. To watch over what is precious to us. To watch over our prayers. To watch over the people mentioned in our prayers—and the fruit we so hope to see.

LESSONS LEARNED

- Part of flourishing is functioning in line with God's design for us and what he has purposed for us to do—and that includes bearing fruit.
- We have all been made in the image of God, but we are so uniquely made. That means God has purposely created us to bear our own specific fruit—and the size, volume, and shape of that fruit will be different for each one of us.
- To produce the fruit we're called to bear will require action on our part, but not the action of frenzied activity. Rather it's the action of living our lives rooted and grounded in God. In fact, the degree to which you are abiding in him is the degree to which you will experience fruitfulness in your life.

QUESTIONS FOR REFLECTION

- Can you identify ways you are currently bearing fruit?
- Can you identify the impact of your fruit?
- How might you feel pressure to compare your fruit to someone else's?

Lesson 13

Accept the Pruning

Staring at the ax blade scars on the trunk of a massive, twisted olive tree in Bosque el Olivar in Lima, Peru, I could only imagine the history the tree had seen. More than two hundred years old, it was young in comparison to the trees it descended from. Yet it had seen the War of Independence when Peru separated from Spain in the early 1800s, and it had the scars to show for it. A forest of three thousand olive trees existed before the war took its toll and loyalists to the Spanish crown began chopping them down by the hundreds, hence the ax scars that remain on the surviving trees to this day.

After the war, caretakers began nourishing the damaged trees that were still standing, making possible the Bosque el Olivar that the people of Lima enjoy today.[1] Though the ax scars remain on many of the trees, there are more than sixteen hundred flourishing olive trees in a working and thriving olive grove in the middle of a park in the city—a sprawling urban area of ten million people—and for the past several years, it has produced ten tons of black olives annually.[2]

Marveling at the trees' beautiful towering canopies, I could see that I had arrived not long after pruning season when branches are trimmed away. None of the trees showed any signs of fruit, but they each had an odd-looking gap cut out of the middle of their canopy. It would have been my preference to have seen them when they were in full bloom, before they bore any fruit, but I was in Lima to speak at a conference that had long been scheduled for this time. Still, I wasn't going to miss visiting this historical olive grove and the park surrounding it.

Talking to one of the park workers through my Spanish interpreter, I discovered that the trees were pruned in the months following the harvest to remove any damaged, diseased, or dying branches. The big opening cut out of the tops was created to let in more airflow—which prevents disease—and so the sunshine could stretch through the limbs to all the leaves. Looking up through the thinned-out branches, I found it reminiscent of an Italian proverb: "Prune each tree so a swallow can fly through the tree without touching its wings."[3] To my untrained eye, I couldn't tell if this was actually the case, but I did realize it was all a necessary cutting away to increase the fruitfulness of the next harvest.[4]

The park worker went on to tell me that olive trees are so resilient that they can handle such pruning even when they are cut farther back, which is sometimes necessary to rejuvenate a tree that's old, neglected, or damaged. *Hard pruning*, it's called.[5] What's even more interesting is that they also cut away plenty of vibrant, living, and fruit-producing branches for the same purpose—so the tree can produce even more fruit the following year.

What surprised me most of all the facts that I discovered about pruning from this enthusiastic and knowledgeable worker was his assertion that no matter how lightly a tree is trimmed or how far back it is cut, the pruning process is *painful* to the tree. Can you imagine? Of course, without a brain or nerves, trees don't have pain receptors or emotions. They don't feel in the same way we do, but they do have reactions. For whatever reason, when they are cut, they will attempt to self-heal. The cells adjacent to the cut will either multiply or grow to cover over the cut.[6]

I don't know every reaction an olive tree experiences when it's cut, but I do know that if a tree isn't pruned, it won't keep producing fruit because pruning stimulates fruit-bearing. And based on all I learned about the trees in Bosque el Olivar, their produce, and how healthy they appeared, it was evident that olive trees need to be pruned regularly.

> If a tree isn't pruned, it won't keep producing fruit because pruning stimulates fruit-bearing.

At the end of our conversation, I couldn't help but think of all the seasons in my life when it felt like God was pruning me, when he was cutting away what was hindering me, holding me back, distracting me, or getting me off course—so I could keep producing fruit that would remain. When he trimmed my relationships, finances, ministry, routines, habits, schedules, and dreams. To this day I can't say that pruning is something I love because there's always a degree of pain and loss involved. But I can say that, in a sense, pruning has had the same effect on me as it has had on all the olive trees surrounding me. Every time God has pruned me, it has been for the purpose of bearing more fruit for his glory.

God, the Master Gardener

Because, like David, we want to be like a flourishing olive tree in the house of God, it is inevitable that we will face times when the branches of our lives will be trimmed or cut back. Pruning is part of the process of us maturing in Christ. Still, I often wish there was another way to grow, a less painful way to flourish. I wish God had a much different way for us to look and act more like him. But Scripture shows us that he is the Master Gardener, who takes to his pruning shears because of his endless love for us, because of all he has planned for us, because he wants us to bear much fruit.

"I am the true vine, and my Father is the gardener," Jesus said. "Every branch in me that does not produce fruit he removes, and he prunes every branch that produces fruit so that it will produce more fruit."[7]

I'll admit that this may be the most painful lesson I learned from the olive tree, as well as the one we typically want to run from. I know I have at times. It's taken me years to recognize that pruning is not punitive but restorative. We aren't pruned because we've done something wrong but because we are being conformed and transformed to the image of Christ. Even Jesus said that we're pruned if we bear fruit *and* pruned if we don't.

It's different from being healed of wounds we experience or uprooting places where bitterness or complacency have taken hold. It's what God does once we are flourishing, once we are growing, once we are bearing much fruit. And just like an olive tree, there is no escape clause for the pruning process. There is no bypassing or avoiding it, not even when we are experiencing great fruitfulness and everything seems to be going well. Like the olive tree, it's part of our growth process while living here on earth.

> Pruning is not punitive but restorative. We aren't pruned because we've done something wrong but because we are being conformed and transformed to the image of Christ.

If you've always seen pruning as negative, then maybe now is the time to reframe your perception of pruning, to see it as a gain rather than a loss—even though sometimes you have to lose in order to gain. The word Jesus used that is translated *prune* is the Greek word *kathairō*. It means "to cleanse," specifically "to prune or purge."[8] When the Master Gardener prunes us, this is what he's after. He's cleansing us; he's purging us; he's eliminating what we don't need for the next season—or he's leading us to do it ourselves. How many times have you felt nudged to prune back your schedule, to eliminate one thing so you can take on another?

When it's God doing the pruning, when he's at work in our lives, he does it tenderly, intentionally, thoughtfully, and carefully because he is our loving Father and he cares for each one of us.[9] I understand that it can still be painful, but we know that God is good and only does good, therefore he only prunes us for our good, whether it feels like it at the time or not.[10] He knows what we need to grow, mature, and become more like him. He knows exactly what needs to be trimmed away to produce an endless supply of fruit all throughout our lives. This is why pruning is an inevitable part of living as disciples of Jesus.[11]

> God is good and only does good, therefore he only prunes us for our good, whether it feels like it at the time or not.

In researching this book, I met olive grove farmers from around the world, and I've shared with you many of my experiences. I have walked with them through their groves in Peru, Morocco, Spain, Greece, Italy, Slovenia, and California—and what I couldn't miss was how every single one loved their groves. I marveled at how they knew each individual tree the way a mother knows a child. They knew which ones were sick, which ones were flourishing, what each one's expected yield would be at harvest time, and which ones would need to be pruned when the last olive was picked. It was evident that with great love and intentionality, after each year's harvest, they picked up their pruning shears and cut off the branches that needed to go, masterfully shaping the canopies. In each instance they were not trying to hurt the trees, though they knew the pruning would hurt, but they understood that a moment of pain facilitated future healthy growth and ensured all the best conditions for an endless supply of fruit, season after season after season.

Choose to Surrender

There are so many similarities between our pruning and the pruning of trees, but there is also a major difference. Trees don't have a will. Trees don't have a volition. They are biologically responsive to the farmer's pruning, but they have no choice in the matter.

We, on the other hand, have a choice. We can respond to the Master Gardener's pruning, and we can reject the Master Gardener's pruning. Rejecting his pruning doesn't mean that we can stop him from pruning us and working for our good as he prunes us, but it does mean we can lose out on the benefits of his pruning.

To reap the full benefits of the Master Gardener's pruning in our lives, we will always need to fully surrender to it, to yield our will to his will. It will always be something we have to choose, and then choose again and again, because the pruning process never ends. It seems that any area where we can grow—or are growing—is an area where we will be pruned.

In my life, nothing has been left unattended to grow wild or become barren for too long, because God is faithful. Yes, I had to yield to the pruning. I had to learn not to fight it. Learn to trust God in it. Especially when I didn't understand what was happening or why, because sometimes it involved people and a difference of opinion. Still, in every instance, because I kept seeking God in it, I came to understand how he was using it to move me forward.

I remember when God led me to start a women's ministry years ago. Amid all the things I didn't know—how, when, the structure, the strategies—what I did know was that he was leading me and calling me to serve in that capacity.

At the same time, there were things I thought I knew that I didn't actually know. I really thought everyone in the world of Christian gatherings for women would be just as thrilled as I was at my new initiative. But as I painfully discovered, that wasn't the case. In many ways, what I envisioned was different from many of the existing paradigms, and as a result, I unexpectedly experienced people I trusted questioning my motives, not inviting me into where I'd once felt welcomed, and even dropping me from group texts and gatherings. I went from being included to no longer being considered "in."

To say it was painful is an understatement. If you've experienced anything like that, then you know. But here is what I can testify to: God wasn't absent. He never is. And even through all I experienced in that season, God continued to prune me so that I wouldn't require the approval of people and I would become totally dependent on his approval. His pruning, as painful as it was at the time, ultimately led to more healing and more freedom for me.

There are times when pruning just seems to happen, and at other times, it's clearly God himself who reaches for the pruning shears. There have been places in the world I called home that I've had to leave, and not just my home country of Australia and all our family and friends there. Sometimes home has been places in my heart where I grew comfortable, where I felt stable, where I was content with the fruit I was producing—and God wanted me to step out of my comfort zone, to stretch, to risk, to be put in a position to trust him more in order to bear even more fruit. Sometimes home has been in the people who once mentored me, nurtured me, and helped me grow. Sometimes it has been in friendships that I nurtured and invested my whole heart into, ones that I didn't move an ocean away from.

Recognizing when God is at work, when he's walking us through detaching from what we so want to be attached to, is part of our maturing process. It's part of letting go of our preconceived ideas of how we think things should be and yielding to his will and plan. It's part of learning to trust him more. When Jesus walked this earth, he modeled for us how to do this. There were times when he, too, had to detach from expectations—expectations that weren't necessarily bad or wrong in and of themselves but had the potential to carry him off course. This even happened with his family.

> While he was still speaking with the crowds, his mother and brothers were standing outside wanting to speak to him. Someone told him, "Look, your mother and your brothers are standing outside, wanting to speak to you."
>
> He replied to the one who was speaking to him, "Who is my mother and who are my brothers?" Stretching out his hand toward his disciples, he said, "Here are my mother and my brothers! For whoever does the will of my Father in heaven is my brother and sister and mother."[12]

Jesus knew how to attach to what was God's will in the present and detach from what would thwart his mission, including what may have been God's will in the past. In my humanity I have to work hard at this, at learning to trust and attach to Jesus more than all the feelings that have tried to overwhelm me. This has been particularly true when I've had to detach from unhealthy attachments to be faithful to follow God—whether they were familial, cultural, spiritual, or professional. And let's just say, for a woman with deep mother wounds resulting from abandonment, adoption, and abuse, this has been no easy process for me. It is only by the power of the Holy Spirit and with the help of counselors and friends that I have been able to find freedom in this tender area of my heart.

What each of us needs to detach from to remain faithful to Jesus may be different from season to season. Still, it is a common, repeating part of the pruning process that we see all throughout

Scripture. The prophets had to detach from the desire to please people with words they wanted to hear.[13] The disciples had to detach from their nets.[14] Matthew had to detach from his tax booth.[15] The women who traveled with them, financially supporting and serving with Jesus, had to detach from cultural roles and norms.[16] Paul had to detach from his reputation and even from self-righteousness.[17] Timothy had to detach from beliefs and biases based on his age.[18]

What will it be for you? Depending on your family's origin, it certainly could be cultural norms. But in truth, it can be any number of things: family traditions, gatherings, or leisure activities. I recently learned of someone who had to detach from their weekly pickleball tournaments to host a Bible study as part of her pruning process. It could really be anything, including other commitments.

Are the moments of surrender in the pruning process painful? Clearly, they are. Almost always. But they are always worth it. Worth it to follow him. Worth it to know him. Worth it to please him. Worth it to be prepared for what he has next. Worth it to bear more fruit for his glory.

We Are Like Olive Trees

Here in this world, master gardeners are people who have been trained to coach communities with their trees and gardens so they flourish. One such master gardener in California has said, "As an aesthetic pruner I look for the trees' essence and beauty, helping them to reveal themselves without compromising their health; finding the thin line between control and nature makes the garden show itself as a unity."[19]

I love this sentiment because it reflects how God prunes us. He sees the end from the beginning. He sees who he created us to be. He sees all the plans and purposes he has for our lives. And he knows how much pruning we can take in every season, and how much pruning we need in order to bear much fruit. After experiencing decades of regular pruning, I promise you that we can trust the Master Gardener with the bigger picture of our lives. We can trust his pruning.

I've made up my mind that I'm going to surrender to all the remaining pruning God has in store for me, no matter how painful. I don't want to resist it. I don't want to start the process and then suddenly stop. I don't want to revert to my old ways in some area, to go back and pick up some branch and try to reattach it.

I know picturing such an idea sounds ridiculous, but we all do it. When we run back to a relationship. When we fall back into old patterns, habits, or attitudes. When we pick back up an offense or unforgiveness. When we do nothing and by default start drifting. I want to keep moving forward. I want to keep growing. I want to keep bearing all the fruit of the Holy Spirit.[20] I want to keep bearing his fruit well into my senior years, because in a world that tells older people, "You are done," God says you can keep bearing fruit until you die. "Planted in the house of the LORD, they [the righteous] thrive in the courts of our God. They will still bear fruit in old age, healthy and green."[21]

We are not supposed to retire or stop when it comes to our spiritual growth, nor are we to grow bitter, cynical, complacent, or grumpy. We're to refire, over and over again with each and every pruning in each and every season. This is how the beauty of our lives is supposed to unfold, no matter our current age. This is more of how we will keep growing and producing much fruit.

LESSONS LEARNED

- It is inevitable that we will face times when the branches of our lives will be trimmed or cut back. Pruning is part of the process of us maturing in Christ.
- Pruning is not punitive but restorative. We are not pruned because we have done something wrong but because we are being conformed and transformed to the image of Christ—and to keep bearing fruit. Even Jesus said that we are pruned if we bear fruit *and* pruned if we don't.
- To reap the full benefits of God's pruning in our lives, we will always need to fully surrender to it, to yield our will to his will. It will always be something we have to choose because the pruning process never ends. It seems that any area where we can grow is an area where we will be pruned.

QUESTIONS FOR REFLECTION

- Can you identify times in the past when you were pruned, whether it was circumstances, God doing the work, or you pruning an area of your life in obedience to God?
- Is there an area of your life God is pruning now?
- Can you identify any areas of your life right now where God wants you to do some pruning?

Lesson 14

Go Through the Press

I've always loved Amsterdam, particularly in the spring. Best known for canals and tulips, the city is also home to the Van Gogh Museum, the Anne Frank House—both of which I've visited several times—and, of course, stroopwafels. As popular to the Dutch as donuts are to the Americans, they're best enjoyed with a fresh, hot cup of coffee.

Nick and I were there in June 2023 at the Amsterdam RAI and the Olympic stadium, where I was giving a keynote address at an international conference focused on evangelism. It was great to catch up with old friends and meet new friends who were as passionate as we are about reaching the lost and taking the gospel to the world. I was definitely in my sweet spot at this gathering, having given almost four decades of my life to evangelism and mission. I was excited that thousands had come together to dream about reaching every person on earth with the gospel.

While sitting in one of the sessions, I started to sense that God was inviting me to step up and assume a more direct role in helping to develop pipelines and pathways to develop young women leaders to serve the church across the globe. I dismissed

the thought as quickly as it had appeared, figuring I was just getting caught up in the inevitable excitement and enthusiasm that
is generated when you put that many passionate people together
in one place and charge them with coming up with a strategy to
take the gospel to the entire world.

As it happened, I was walking across a parking lot later when
the leader of the organization hosting the conference stopped me
and said, "Chris, I feel that you are supposed to initiate a women's
alliance as a part of this movement." I almost fell over right there
in that parking lot because that is what I had felt the Lord was
asking of me during the meeting.

That night I wrestled with God in my hotel room because
I knew the cost of saying yes. I had said yes many times before:
when Nick and I started Equip & Empower Ministries, when we
founded A21, when we initiated Propel, and everything that has
come since from all three of those global initiatives. I was already
committed to the work before me, and Nick and I were soon to
be empty nesters, so my plan was to spend a little more time
together on a Greek island like we did on our honeymoon—not
to start a new initiative.

If I said yes, it would have a significant impact on the development of young women leaders, but it would also require great
sacrifice and a huge investment of my time, energy, resources,
and attention. I know what it means to feel pressed, and I
knew this would mean pressing on multiple fronts. Every kingdom assignment always does. There's the pressing *upon* as the
increased load is applied. There's the pressing *into* seeking God
and being responsive to what he wants to press into me—as he
is always in the process of conforming us into the image of his
Son. There's the pressing *against* the status quo as new ground

is contested. And certainly, there's the being pressed *against* by spiritual opposition.

I had to decide whether I was prepared to pay the price of pressing on—which would mean consciously exerting a steady force against things like ease, routine, comfort, complacency, safety, the status quo, and security—or choosing to coast into retirement and accept that my best days were behind me instead of in front of me.

It seems like a no-brainer on this side of that decision, but I can assure you that I felt the weight of being willing to go into another season of pressing so that fresh oil could flow from my life and be poured into another generation. It has been more than a year since I said yes to leading that global initiative, and it's showing to be the most fruitful and satisfying season of my life. Creating ecosystems for developing women leaders all over the globe is astounding and deeply fulfilling—and it will result in fruit being produced long after I am gone.

Olives Have to Be Pressed

One of the major lessons I have learned from the olive tree I shared in one of my previous books:

> To get flavorful, robust extra virgin olive oil (EVOO), olives have to be pressed. . . . They have to endure being transformed from one state into another. . . . To give you an idea of what I mean, initially, after olives are harvested from the trees, they are quickly cleaned and pressed into a paste, pits and all— either with an ancient method of a grinding wheel weighing

hundreds of pounds or with modern industrial equipment. The paste is spread onto fibrous cloths that are layered one on top of the other, where they are pressed even more with pounds and pounds of pressure so intense that every drop of oil is squeezed out.

But even after all that, the oil goes through another kind of pressing. It's heated—just high enough but not too high—so the impurities fall to the bottom and the EVOO rises to the top. It's silky, beautifully colored, and ready to be stored where it can rest. Much like the taste-testing of a fine wine, the olive oil is tasted to ensure its quality. Later, when it has rested long enough, it is bottled into green or dark-colored glass—the perfect color to block harmful UV rays that can spoil it.

The best-tasting olive oil is made when the olives are picked at just the right time, crushed quickly into a paste, pressed again at just the right intervals, heated to just the right temperature, cooled for just the right amount of time, and then bottled at the right moment. No doubt, to make the perfect bottle of oil requires the right amount of pressing at all the right times.[1]

That is quite a process, and I am pretty sure that if you asked an olive at any point during the process if the pressing was good for it, it would categorically say, "No!" (Don't worry; even though my Greek self is obsessed with olives, I have never tried to talk to them.)

Unless. Unless the olive knew something about the one picking it. Unless it knew something about the one crushing it. Unless it knew something about the one heating it. Unless it knew something about the one bottling it. Unless it knew that there was good and more in mind for it—including a broader and longer-lasting use than simply hanging on the tree.

You see, from the time an olive is first starting to form until the time it is harvested is about five to eight months. That olive on a tree has a singular use: It serves as food.[2] But as EVOO, it can last for as long as eighteen to twenty-four months unopened. And once opened, its shelf life can be extended even further through proper storage. As we all know, olive oil can be used in countless ways. But whatever its use, an olive only becomes oil through the precise and prolonged process of pressing.

God knows what we need and when we need it to become more resilient.

I would venture to say our spiritual lives are much the same. God knows what we need and when we need it to become more resilient. To grow. To mature. To become more like Christ. He knows what we need to be transformed and to surrender more of our will for his will. He knows what we need to have fresh oil so we can keep flourishing and producing more fruit. He knows what we need to keep walking in all his plans and purposes for our lives. And none of us are exempt from this process. Even Jesus didn't get a pass from pressing when he walked this earth. He knew better than any of us ever will what it means to go through the press.

When Jesus was facing the hardest decision of his life, he was in the Garden of Gethsemane, which is an olive grove. Even more interesting is that *Gethsemane* literally means "oil press" in

Hebrew.[3] Located at the foot of the Mount of Olives, this garden is where he wrestled in prayer before going to the cross, to the point he sweated drops of blood.[4]

The imagery of all this isn't lost on me, and I imagine it's not lost on you either. There in the garden Jesus endured a type of soul anguish we can never know, but his experience helps us understand the value of choosing what God wants over what we want every time we're faced with such a choice.

Jesus knew that he was about to be tried, rejected, and condemned to death by the very people he came to save. He knew the intense physical pain he was about to endure when he would be crucified. He knew that our sin was about to be imputed to him on the cross.[5] He knew that for the first time in eternity, there would be a breach in the unbroken fellowship he had enjoyed with his Father. The thoughts of what he was about to endure literally overwhelmed his mind and heart. At one point he fell to the ground and began praying, "Father, if you are willing, take this cup away from me—nevertheless, not my will, but yours, be done."[6]

What was Jesus saying when he prayed this? Was he at odds with and opposed to the desires of the Father in this moment? Did he want one thing and the Father want another? It can certainly seem like that on the surface. But there is a key in the Greek that reveals otherwise, and that key is that there are two different words for *will* in this passage.

In this prayer when Jesus said, "If you are willing," the first word for *will* is the Greek word *boulomai*. It refers to God's "purposed or fixed will." In the second use of the word *will*, when Jesus said, "Nevertheless, not my will," it's the Greek word *theléma*. It refers to God's "preferred or desired will."[7]

This is so significant! Why? Because when we don't know

that there are two different words for *will*—*boulomai* versus *theléma*—and when we focus only on the second part of Jesus's phrase and overlook the first part, what ends up happening? We're apt to end up reading the second phrase out of context and possibly end up believing that what Jesus wanted and what the Father wanted were substantively different.

But when we are aware of the presence and significance of both words for *will* and take into account Jesus's condition for his request—that he only wanted the cup to be removed if that was compatible with the Father's purposed will—making a way for salvation, all of a sudden we understand that what looks like a contradiction on the surface is a singular desire. The Father's *preferred* will is what accomplishes his *purposed* will. And being one in purpose with the Father, Jesus's preferred will was to accomplish the same.

The bottom line is that when Jesus prayed this prayer, he wasn't opposing the Father's purposed will because the Father's purposed will was Jesus's purposed will too. Rather, when Jesus prayed this prayer, he was saying that his preference would be to accomplish that purpose by another means if such a means existed, but it didn't. But either way, Jesus was clear that what he wanted most, above all, was the Father's purpose.

I have prayed prayers like this many times. I imagine that you have too. And it's a prayer I imagine we will all find ourselves praying again and again as we find ourselves in our Gethsemanes, in our places of pressing. Yet if we follow in Jesus's footsteps, if we prize and pursue God's purposed will and way above our preferred will and way in that place, God will produce fresh oil through the pressing and lead us to flourish, even though there is often great pain in that process.

Pressing Is Painful

When I was in my early twenties, I was in a relationship with someone I loved dearly, and I wanted to spend the rest of my life with this person. The problem was that this person was not a follower of Jesus, and our relationship was far from godly. There was simply no way that I could live the life God was calling me to live and remain in that relationship.

Every ounce of my being wanted to stay with this person, but I remember clearly the night when I had to make a decision one way or another. I couldn't see what was ahead; I could not have imagined all that God would do in and through my life through that one act of obedience. All I knew was that I was absolutely terrified of losing the one thing that, at the time, I loved more than anything else. But I said those words: "Nevertheless, not my will, but yours, be done."

It was not easy to walk out of that relationship—in fact it was the hardest thing I ever did in my life. Afterward, I went through great heartache and loss, as well as living with the fact that I had deeply hurt that person. But that time of pressing prepared me for all that God had for me. It was probably the beginning of my learning to walk in the Spirit the way God intended: "I say, then, walk by the Spirit and you will certainly not carry out the desire of the flesh. For the flesh desires what is against the Spirit, and the Spirit desires what is against the flesh; these are opposed to each other, so that you don't do what you want."[8]

When I look back now, I can see God's amazing grace and mercy in my life. Had I stayed in that relationship, I wouldn't have met and married Nick. There would be no A21 or Propel Women or Equip & Empower Ministries. No global evangelism initiative. All the fruit of these past thirty-five years would never have come to pass if I hadn't submitted to the will of God for my life at that time.

Yes, I felt heartbroken and devastated. I did not think I would survive that season, but it was that very pressing through obedience that produced the oil that has enabled my life to bear fruit for the glory of God.

I could tell you numerous other stories throughout my journey that have the same thread of surrender in them. In order to fulfill the purpose of God for my life and to step into the promises of God, I have had to constantly choose to surrender my will to God's will. And the same is true for you. The pathway to true joy, true fulfillment, true freedom is via Gethsemane, again and again. Of course, none of us will ever have to endure what Jesus did that night in the olive grove, but every single day we will be faced with decisions about relationships, finances, careers, lifestyles, habits, or priorities. And when we do, what will we choose as we respond to God's speaking through his Word and by his Spirit?

When God says go, will we go?
When God says stay, will we stay?
When God says stop, will we stop?
When God says run, will we run?
When God says wait, will we wait?

Will we follow where God leads when it makes sense? And what about when it doesn't? When it seems to come with blessing and benefit? What about when it comes with cost and loss?

What about when what God calls us to isn't what we hoped

for, isn't what we wanted, isn't what we like, or isn't what we dreamed? What will we do then?

I know that choices in these moments of decision are never easy and often painful. But every single one of them, that we no doubt will have to make over and over in our lives, leads to flourishing. They lead to having the fresh oil we need in our lives to do all that God has called us to do.

It's Time to Trust

In order to be able to pray, "Nevertheless, not what I will, but what you will," we have to believe in the marrow of our bones that God is good, that his purposes are good, and that even when we experience the effects of sin—which is not good—he is at work to redeem it all for our good.[9]

God doesn't withhold abundant life from us. Quite the contrary: Jesus came that we might have life more abundant.[10] It's just that the path to abundant life is often at odds with our desires and understanding. I know that we think we know what's best for us, but it's God who knows. He loves us. He is for us. He created us. He is not trying to limit, contain, or frustrate us. He is the one who wants us to flourish and thrive more than we do.

The challenge for us is whether we are willing to trust him and his ways above our own thoughts and our own ways. Isaiah reminds us: "'For my thoughts are not your thoughts, and your ways are not my ways.' This is the LORD's declaration. 'For as heaven is higher than earth, so my ways are higher than your ways, and my thoughts than your thoughts.'"[11]

We need to ask ourselves, Are we willing to trust God even when we don't quite understand why he is asking us to do something or to give something up? Are we willing to believe he knows what's best for us? Are we willing to trust his timing and his ways? Proverbs reminds us: "Trust in the LORD with all your heart, and do not rely on your own understanding; in all your ways know him, and he will make your paths straight."[12]

Faith is predicated on trust rather than understanding, so we need to put our trust in God during our Gethsemane moments. And with that trust, we need to run to him and pour out our heart to him just like Jesus did. When Jesus prayed to the Father, he did not pray a nice polite prayer; he fell to the ground and cried out to God. He passionately prayed, saying the same thing three different times: "Take this cup away from me. Nevertheless, not what I will, but what you will."[13]

So many of us fear our Gethsemane moments not because we doubt God's faithfulness and goodness but because we believe we will leave Gethsemane with less. But that isn't what happened to Jesus. What's more, he didn't leave the same either. He left changed and with gain, strengthened by the Father's presence and strengthened for the Father's purposes. Jesus waged and won the war of greatest eternal significance in Gethsemane on the soil of surrender. And wars of eternal significance are still waged in the same place today.

The lesson of the olive tree is that no matter how mature a tree becomes, it will always have more fruit to bear, and therefore, there will always be more olives to pick and more pressing to be done. No matter how far God has brought you, he isn't done with you yet. There is more he wants to do in you and through you. Whatever it is that you're wrestling with that you don't want to die to, give up, or walk away from, go to Gethsemane in confidence. Trust in God's goodness, knowing he is the same yesterday, today, and forever.[14] Believe he will meet with you there as he met with Jesus.

> The lesson of the olive tree is that no matter how mature a tree becomes, it will always have more fruit to bear.

Whether God is asking you to give something up or to press on when you'd rather coast, like I wrestled with in Amsterdam, continuing to produce fresh oil requires consistent surrender—dying to self, taking up your cross, and following Jesus.[15] There are no shortcuts; there is only daily surrender and making the decision that we are going to run our race and finish our course.[16] We never arrive on this side of eternity. We want to be faithful to the end. We want to be rooted and resilient to the end. We want to endure to the end. We want to bear much fruit to bring God great glory to the end.

LESSONS LEARNED

- God knows what we need and when we need it to grow. To mature. To become more like Christ.
- God knows what we need to be transformed and to surrender more of our will for his will, to produce more fresh oil.
- We all have our Gethsemane moments and prayers when we surrender more of our will for his will.

QUESTIONS FOR REFLECTION

- When was the last time you prayed a Gethsemane prayer?
- Is there something you had to give up? What was it?
- What are you wrestling with right now that God wants you to surrender to him?

Epilogue

The Olive Tree, an Enduring Evergreen

But I am like a flourishing olive tree in the house of God;
I trust in God's faithful love forever and ever.
PSALM 52:8

Just when I thought I had uncovered all there was to know about the olive tree, I discovered something new on a recent trip to Southeast Asia to visit our A21 teams. And of course I wanted to share it with you—hence I had to add an epilogue.

There in Southeast Asia, where I least expected it, I was thrilled to discover there are Chinese olive trees that fall under the botanical name *Canarium album*. They are different from the European varietals we've discussed thus far, the ones that fall under the botanical name *Olea europaea*, but they are indeed olive-producing trees. I don't know if this means the two are cousins or not, but it made me so happy to know that some kind of olive tree also grows in that part of the world.

Chinese olive trees produce flowers with a pink center—and they are breathtaking. The fruit the flower produces is a deep black color when harvested. Though Chinese olives are typically not pressed for oil, after they are soaked in brine they can be cooked in dishes or eaten as a snack.[1] They can be dried or processed into candy, beverages, jams, or wine.[2] What's more, their leaves differ from the silvery, leathery varietals of Mediterranean climates. Instead, they are a bright green, some with ruffled edges. God is so creative in everything he made, isn't he?

What I appreciated most about the Chinese olive trees is that, like their European counterparts, they are evergreens—trees that symbolize life, resilience, and growth. Evergreens are often associated with strength, endurance, and adaptability because of their ability to thrive in various climates and conditions. They are physically characterized as slow molting, meaning they replace leaves as they lose them so their appearance is lush, green foliage all year round.[3]

When fall and winter come for other trees, when they start changing colors and brilliant yellows, oranges, and reds fade into brown, when they begin dropping leaves and are left standing naked, evergreens remain green. When other trees grow dormant, evergreens continue providing shelter, protection, and food for insects, birds, and small animals.[4] Despite seasons of drought or excessive rain; despite seasons of high temperatures or deep freezes; despite humidity, storms, or wind, they appear the same. Green. Flourishing. Beautiful. Full. And in the case of our beloved olive tree, fruitful.

Since we are called to be like olive trees, then it stands to reason that we are also called to be like evergreens—and to live an evergreen life as long as God has us on this earth. An evergreen life is one where we stay green and flourishing despite the external conditions surrounding us. It's based on living out of the eternal life God has given us. In the words of Jeremiah, "The person who trusts in the LORD, whose confidence indeed is the LORD, is blessed. He will be like a tree planted by water: it sends its roots out toward a stream, it doesn't fear when heat comes, and its foliage remains green. It will not worry in a year of drought or cease producing fruit."[5]

If we are flourishing when surrounded by the same pain, suffering, injustice, chaos, and confusion as everyone else, then it will cause people to wonder what is different about us. We may be living on earth alongside everyone else, but because we are abiding in Christ, we can be producing fruit—like love, joy, peace, patience, goodness, kindness, gentleness, faithfulness, and self-control—no matter how dry, barren, chaotic, confusing, and terrifying the world is around us. Because we live an evergreen life in Christ, we can provide shade, protection, and nutrition to those within our spheres of influence. We can be green and flourishing in all seasons. This is what lessons from the olive tree have shown us in so many ways.

Isaiah wrote, "I will put in the desert the cedar and the acacia, the myrtle and the olive. I will set junipers in the wasteland, the fir and the cypress together."[6] Every tree listed in this verse is an evergreen, and every one of them is designed to signal the location of water sources and provide shade in the desert.[7] What an image of how God made us to be in this world—people who are evergreen, who can share with others living water, a life-giving moment, a place to find refuge and hope.

It's not lost on me that other than God and people, the Bible mentions trees more than any other living thing. Every significant theological event is marked by a tree—or some part of a tree.[8] It's the most-used metaphor in Scripture.[9] In fact, in more than a thousand texts, trees are used to illustrate life and growth, testing and decision-making, connecting to God, and our eternal life.[10] But no one tree is referenced more than the olive tree when you include all its derivatives—olives, olive wood, olive oil, olive branches, and olive groves. There are more than two hundred references to all things olive tree.[11] No wonder the olive tree has taught us so much.

Together, we have learned how to anchor our roots down deep in our spiritual relationship with God and to spread them in every direction in relationships with others. How to behold over and over the beauty of God in all his majesty. How to have hope in the face of none. How to allow God and his Word to influence every area of our lives. How to walk in true humility in a world all about self. How to walk in the fresh oil of the Holy Spirit and take everything to him in prayer. How to stay in a place of peace in a world full of chaos. How to stand up for injustice whenever we see it or experience it. How to stay green and flourish through every season. And how to flourish and bear fruit in every age and stage of our lives. All lessons for living an evergreen life in a world desperate for it.

In the last decade there's been such a shaking in the world and in the church, and we have all felt it. When Israel broke its covenant with God, Jeremiah wrote in one breath, "The LORD named you a flourishing olive tree, beautiful with well-formed fruit," and in the next, "He has set fire to it, and its branches are consumed with the sound of a mighty tumult."[12] It's shocking how fast things can change. I don't imagine the shaking has ended, as the writer of Hebrews said that everything that can be shaken will be shaken so that only what can't be shaken will remain.[13]

Even now, things look bleak. Wars are raging. Natural disasters are decimating entire communities. Fear and insecurity govern our world politically and economically. Chaos and confusion are running rampant. With access to 24/7 news cycles on our phones, we might feel that this is the worst time in history and that it has never been this bad before, but it has all been this way since the fall. The disobedience that brought about the consequences of the fall is still at work today. And the darkness, the distancing from God, the ache, the pain, the evil, and the suffering that followed the fall are still at work today too. They are real. They are present. They are unavoidable, and they are inescapable. For now.

But none of them have the final word. Only he who is the Word has the final word, and his Word is that this time is not forever. Rather, a day is coming for those who are in him—a day when death will be put to death, a day when sin and all its consequences will cease, a day when all will be set right again with his people abiding in his presence and peace permanently.

Still, as we look for and wait for that day, God is ever faithful. He has not abandoned us, but he has given us his precious Holy Spirit, and his kingdom is already breaking into this world. So as we look and long for that day, we wait in hope, strengthened by his Spirit and steadfast in his promises: "Evergreens will grow in place of thorn bushes, firs will grow in place of nettles; they will be a monument to the LORD, a permanent reminder that will remain."[14]

We are like the evergreens! We are like the olive trees! And it's what we have learned from the olive tree that helps us navigate the present and the future, that reminds us how to thrive in the midst of it all, that helps us stay green and bear fruit regardless of the thorns and thistles that crop up in our world. It's the olive tree that reminds us to stay connected to God, living out the eternal life he has given us. As you close this book, my prayer is that you return to it again and again because the lessons of the olive tree are as evergreen as the olive tree itself. They are water. They are life. They are God's enduring wisdom to us. They are his design for a flourishing, rooted, resilient, and fruitful life!

LOVE,

Acknowledgments

I am so deeply grateful to every person who has helped to ensure that *The Faith to Flourish: God's Design for a Rooted, Resilient, and Fruitful Life* made it from a revelation on the Acropolis in Athens, Greece, to become the book you're holding now.

Without my mother's inspiration—and her love for olive oil—this book wouldn't be all that it is. *Thank you Catherine Caryofyllis* for your obsession with olive oil. To say it marked me is an understatement. *Nick, Catherine, and Sophia*, you are always there in the writing process, in the stories and life experiences we have shared. *Elizabeth Prestwood*, you are truly the world's best collaborative writer, and we had so much fun researching and writing all things olive tree. *Rebekah Layton*, there are not enough words to express my gratitude for your willingness to review every lesson from the olive tree and offer profound wisdom and insight that made this a better book than it otherwise would have been.

To our A21, Propel, Zoe Church, and Equip & Empower teams, volunteers, partners, and supporters: What you all do every day is extraordinary. Serving Jesus alongside you is the greatest privilege and honor of my life. Let's keep changing the world together, one life at a time. I love you all. *Mattie Meese, your creative input and commitment to every last detail of this project is a gift.*

To the team at Nelson Books: Andrew Stoddard, Chris Sigfrids, Hanha Parham, Natalie Nyquist, Jamekra Willis, Claire Drake, Lisa Beech, Darren Samuel, and Kristy Edwards—and to the team at Yates & Yates, namely Matt and Karen Yates: Thank you for believing in the message of this book and all you did to help it come to life. Each of you poured your heart and soul into this project.

To every olive grove farmer and olive oil producer I met in Peru, Morocco, Spain, Greece, Italy, Slovenia, California, and Southeast Asia: Thank you for letting me come spend time in your groves with your beloved olive trees. Thank you for letting me ask endless questions. Thank you for letting me see your processes—and taste your olive oil. Thank you for letting me see your love for the olive tree—and for teaching me to love it the way you do. I couldn't have learned all I did without you. *To Michael O'Hara Garcia and the Florida Olive Council:* Thank you for generously sharing your years of hard work and scientific research growing olive trees. Your contributions are evident throughout this book.

To my Lord and Savior, Jesus Christ: Because of your goodness, I, too, am like a flourishing olive tree in your house; I trust in your faithful love forever and ever (Psalm 52:8).

Notes

Introduction: The Sacred Olive Tree

1. Editors of the Encyclopaedia Britannica, "Athena," *Encyclopaedia Britannica*, last updated March 20, 2025, https://www.britannica.com/topic/Athena-Greek-mythology.

2. Philip Crysopoulos, "Parthenon Voted the World's Most Beautiful Building," *Greek Reporter*, May 29, 2018, https://greekreporter.com/2018/05/29/parthenon-voted-worlds-most-beautiful-building/.

3. Evan Hadingham, "Unlocking Mysteries of the Parthenon," *Smithsonian Magazine*, February 2008, https://www.smithsonianmag.com/history/unlocking-mysteries-of-the-parthenon-16621015/.

4. Natalie Martin, "The Ancient, Sacred Olive Tree of the Acropolis That Never Dies," *Greek City Times*, June 27, 2021, https://greekcitytimes.com/2021/06/27/olive-tree-acropolis/.

5. Martin, "Ancient, Sacred Olive Tree."

6. Martin, "Ancient, Sacred Olive Tree."

7. Psalm 52:8.

8. ESV.

9. Vincent van Gogh, *Olive Grove*, 1889, oil on canvas, 73.2 x 92.2 cm, Van Gogh Museum, Amsterdam, https://www.vangoghmuseum.nl/en/collection/s0045v1962.

10. Regina Gagnon, "The Two Olive Trees," *Great Works of Literature I (Fall 2016)*, September 6, 2016, https://blogs.baruch .cuny.edu/greatworks2016/?p=179.

11. "Olive Branch Petition," American Battlefield Trust, accessed March 25, 2025, https://www.battlefields.org/learn/primary -sources/olive-branch-petition.

12. "How Olive Oil Became Europe's 'Liquid Gold,'" Great Italian Chefs, October 11, 2019, https://www.greatitalianchefs.com /features/history-of-olive-oil.

Lesson 1: Root Yourself in God's Love

1. Rick Steves, "Italy's Riviera: Cinque Terre," posted May 18, 2015, by Rick Steve's Europe, YouTube, 25:04, https://www.youtube .com/watch?v=WP316ABiTt0; Amy Inman, "Help Save Cinque Terre's Stone Walls," *Italy Magazine*, February 17, 2020, https://www.italymagazine.com/featured-story/help-save -cinque-terres-stone-walls.

2. "How Long Can an Olive Tree Live?," *Chateau de Luz*, accessed March 26, 2025, https://www.chateaudeluz.com/blogs/learn /how-long-can-an-olive-tree-live; Daphne Chouliaraki Milner, "Trees for the Ages: The Wisdom of Greece's Olive Growers," *Atmos*, September 16, 2024, https://atmos.earth/trees-for-the -ages-the-wisdom-of-greeces-olive-growers/.

3. "The Magnificent European Olive Tree," Land Arch Concepts, accessed April 16, 2025, https://landarchconcepts.wordpress. com/the-magnificent-european-olive-tree/; Kiersten Rankel, "All About Your Olive Tree's Roots," Greg, July 20, 2024, https://greg .app/olive-tree-roots/.

4. "8 Amazing Attributes of Olive Trees That Will Humble and Inspire You," *Olive My Pickle*, accessed April 9, 2025, https:// www.olivemypickle.com/blogs/news/8-amazing-attributes-of -olive-trees-that-will-humble-and-inspire-you; "Olive Trees," Forno Bravo, accessed April 16, 2025, https://www.fornobravo .com/olive-oil/olive-trees/olive-trees-1/.

5. Job 14:7–9.

6. *Merriam-Webster Dictionary*, "root," accessed March 30, 2025, https://www.merriam-webster.com/dictionary/root; "rooting," Dictionary.com, accessed March 30, 2025, https://www.dictionary.com/browse/rooting.

7. "rooted," Dictionary.com, accessed March 30, 2025, https://www.dictionary.com/browse/rooted.

8. Colossians 2:6–7.

9. *New Testament Greek Lexicon: New American Standard*, "Rhizoo Meaning," Bible Study Tools, accessed March 29, 2025, https://www.biblestudytools.com/lexicons/greek/nas/rhizoo.html.

10. Mike Leake, "What Does Colossians 2:6–7 Teach Us About Our Faith Walk?," Bible Study Tools, April 27, 2023, https://www.biblestudytools.com/bible-study/topical-studies/what-does-colossians-26-7-teach-us-about-our-faith-walk.html.

11. Romans 11:17.

12. Irene Julca et al., "Genomic Evidence for Recurrent Genetic Admixture During the Domestication of Mediterranean Olive Trees (*Olea europaea* L.)," *BMC Biology* 18, no. 148 (2020), https://doi.org/10.1186/s12915-020-00881-6.

13. Mark McWhorter, "The Grafted Olive Tree," The Old Paths Bible School, 2002, http://www.oldpaths.org/Classes/Children/WC/Stories/wc06_15.html.

14. Galatians 3:26, 29.

15. Genesis 12:2–3 NASB1995.

16. Deuteronomy 7:6.

17. Exodus 4:22.

18. Jeremiah 11:16.

19. Brittany Allen, "What Does It Mean to Be a Child of God?," Well-Watered Women Co., June 27, 2023, https://wellwateredwomen.com/what-does-it-mean-to-be-a-child-of-god/.

20. Outline of verses and blessings from Allen, "What Does It Mean to Be a Child of God?"

21. Isaiah 63:16.

22. Psalm 119:68; Luke 18:18–19.
23. Ephesians 1:5–6.
24. Matthew 3:17, 17:5.
25. "Accepted in the Beloved," Precept Austin, last updated January 21, 2021, https://www.preceptaustin.org/accepted_in_the_beloved; John 19:30.
26. Matthew 27:46.
27. "Accepted in the Beloved," Precept Austin.
28. Romans 8:38–39.
29. Philip Renner, "What God Thinks About You," Renner Ministries, accessed April 16, 2025, https://renner.org/article/what-god-thinks-about-you/.
30. Genesis 1:27; Ephesians 2:10.
31. 2 Corinthians 6:18.
32. 1 Peter 2:9.
33. John 15:4–7 NKJV.
34. Robert E. Stewart, "Fertilizer," *Encyclopaedia Britannica*, last updated March 26, 2025, https://www.britannica.com/topic/fertilizer.
35. Psalm 52:8.
36. Romans 12:2.
37. Psalm 52:8.

Lesson 2: Behold the Beauty of God

1. Psalm 52:8.
2. Hosea 14:6 AMPC.
3. Psalm 8.
4. "What Is 'Nature Deficit Disorder,' and Can the Outdoors Really Make Us Feel Better?," HealthPartners, accessed March 27, 2025, https://www.healthpartners.com/blog/nature-deficit-disorder/.
5. Romans 1:20.
6. Psalm 27:4.
7. "A Meditation on Psalm 27:4—Gaze," Warren Church, accessed

March 28, 2025, https://warren.church/wow/a-meditation-on
-psalm-274-gaze/.

8. *Merriam-Webster Dictionary*, "gaze," accessed March 28, 2025,
https://www.merriam-webster.com/dictionary/gaze.

9. Colossians 1:15.

10. Isaiah 53:2.

11. J. A. Medders, "God Is Beautiful. It's Not Weird," *Spiritual
Theology*, December 9, 2020, https://www.spiritualtheology.net
/god-is-beautiful-its-not-weird/.

12. 2 Corinthians 3:18.

13. 2 Corinthians 3:18.

14. 2 Corinthians 4:7.

15. Romans 12:15.

16. Hosea 14:6 AMPC.

Lesson 3: Nourish Your Heart

1. Mavroudis Family, "Olive Grove Environment and Natural
Biodiversity," Mavroudis Olive Oil, accessed April 16, 2025,
https://oliveoilcorfu.gr/olive-grove-enviroment-natural
-biodiversity/.

2. Mavroudis, "Olive Grove Environment"; David Feela, "Neighbors
Who Visit My Backyard in the Dead of Night," *High Country
News*, April 23, 2014, https://www.hcn.org/wotr/neighbors
-who-visit-my-backyard-in-the-dead-of-night/.

3. Seth L. Scott, "Why Does the Bible Say Out of the Abundance of
the Heart the Mouth Speaks?," Christianity.com, November 8,
2023, https://www.christianity.com/wiki/bible/out-of-the
-abundance-of-the-heart-his-mouth-speaks.html.

4. Daniel L. Akin and Jonathan Akin, *Christ-Centered Exposition:
Exalting Jesus in Proverbs*, eds. David Platt et al. (B&H
Publishing, 2017), 68–72.

5. Clarence L. Hayes Jr., "Why and How to Guard Your Heart
Above All Else," Crosswalk, October 25, 2023, https://www

.crosswalk.com/faith/bible-study/why-should-we-guard-our
-hearts-according-to-proverbs.html.

6. Proverbs 23:7 NKJV.

7. Mark 12:30.

8. Romans 10:9–10.

9. Mark 7:21–23.

10. Alejandra O'Connell-Domenech, "Why More Americans Are Going to Therapy," The Hill, May 1, 2023, https://thehill.com /policy/healthcare/3975996-why-more-americans-are-going -to-therapy/.

11. Proverbs 4:23.

12. Matthew 13:3–9.

13. *Merriam-Webster Dictionary*, "guard," accessed March 31, 2025, https://www.merriam-webster.com/dictionary/guard.

14. "Guards at Windsor," The Household Division, accessed March 31, 2025, https://www.householddivision.org.uk /changing-the-guard-overview.

15. *Merriam-Webster Dictionary*, "stand guard / watch," accessed March 31, 2025, https://www.merriam-webster.com/dictionary /stand%20guard%2Fwatch.

16. William David Reyburn and Euan McG. Fry, *A Handbook on Proverbs*, UBS Handbook Series (United Bible Societies, 2000), 112.

17. Jeremiah 17:9 ESV.

18. Matthew 16:24, 6:33.

19. 1 Samuel 13:14; Acts 13:22.

20. *Merriam-Webster Dictionary*, "uproot," accessed April 16, 2025, https://www.merriam-webster.com/dictionary/uproot.

21. John 15:8.

22. Jeremian 1:10 NIV.

23. Psalm 52:8.

24. Alyson Maticic, "Why Is My Olive Tree Dying? [And What to Do About It]," Garden Tabs, July 21, 2022, https://gardentabs .com/why-olive-tree-dying-what-to-do/; Noah Agles, "How to

Tell If Olive Tree Is Dead [And How to Revive It]," Garden Tabs, April 30, 2023, https://gardentabs.com/olive-tree-dead/.

25. Psalm 34:18.
26. Psalm 147:3.
27. Hebrews 10:23.

Lesson 4: Pursue Slow, Steady Growth

1. Vangelis Kleft, "15 Interesting Facts About Olive Tree," Oliviada, accessed April 16, 2025, https://www.oliviadaolive.com/facts -about-olive-tree/; Ray Vander Laan, "Olive Trees," That the World May Know, accessed April 16, 2025, https://www .thattheworldmayknow.com/olive-trees; "Frequently Asked Questions About Growing Olive Trees," My Olive Tree, December 28, 2021, https://www.myolivetree.com/frequently -asked-questions-about-growing-olive-trees/.
2. Ken Goldstein, "The Janka Hardness Test for Hardwoods," *The Electronic Journals of Martial Arts and Sciences*, accessed March 31, 2025, https://ejmas.com/tin/2009tin/tinart_goldstein _0904.html.
3. 1 Kings 6:23–28, 31–33.
4. "Olive Wood—Characteristics, Uses, Benefits," Wood Assistant, accessed March 31, 2025, http://www.woodassistant.com/wood -database/olive-wood/.
5. Dr. Henry Cloud, *Boundaries for Leadership: Results, Relationships, and Being Ridiculously in Charge* (HarperCollins, 2013), 84.
6. Luke 2:41–50, 3:23.
7. Luke 2:40.
8. Luke 2:52.
9. Chad Brand et al., eds., "Increase" in *Holman Illustrated Bible Dictionary* (Holman Bible Publishers, 2003), 816.
10. Faithlife, "Wisdom (knowledge)," *Logos Bible Study Bible Sense Lexicon*, Logos Bible Study software, accessed April 14, 2025, https://www.logos.com/.

11. Deuteronomy 4:6; Proverbs 1:7.
12. Faithlife, "Stature (*hélikia*)," *Logos Bible Study Bible Sense Lexicon*; Brand et al., "Stature" in *Holman Illustrated Bible Dictionary*, 1533.
13. Ephesians 4:13; "Stature," Bible Hub, accessed April 17, 2025, https://biblehub.com/topical/s/stature.htm.
14. Matthew 6:27; Luke 12:25; Brand et al., "Stature."
15. Jake Wyatt, "The Handling of the Truth," Sermons by Logos, accessed April 17, 2025, https://sermons.logos.com/sermons /1205256-%22the-handling-of-the-truth%22.
16. "The Concept of Favor," Bible Hub, accessed April 17, 2025, https://biblehub.com/topical/t/the_concept_of_favor.htm.
17. Ephesians 4:13.
18. Ephesians 4:15.
19. Philippians 1:9.
20. 1 Timothy 4:15.
21. 1 Peter 2:2.
22. 2 Peter 3:18.
23. *Merriam-Webster Dictionary*, "posture," accessed April 1, 2025, https://www.merriam-webster.com/dictionary/posture.
24. Philippians 2:13.
25. Philippians 1:6 NKJV.

Lesson 5: Cultivate Humility

1. Romans 11:17–18.
2. *Merriam-Webster Dictionary*, "boast," accessed April 1, 2025, https://www.merriam-webster.com/dictionary/boast.
3. Proverbs 3:7; Isaiah 5:21; Romans 1:22, 12:16.
4. Chris Witts, "A Lesson in Humility—Part 1—Morning Devotions," Hope 103.2, January 14, 2025, https://hope1032.com .au/stories/faith/devotions/2021/lesson-humility-part-1-4/.
5. Gary Hardin, "Humility," in *Holman Illustrated Bible Dictionary*, ed. Chad Brand et al. (Holman Bible Publishers, 2003), 792.

6. *Oxford English Dictionary*, "entitlement (n.)," March 2025, https://doi.org/10.1093/OED/4835174675.

7. John 15:5.

8. Hebrews 2:3 NKJV.

9. A. W. Tozer, *Man, The Dwelling Place of God* (Christian Publications, 1961), 27.

10. Zephaniah 2:3.

11. Colossians 3:12.

12. Philippians 2:3–4.

13. Philippians 2:6–8.

14. James 4:6.

15. 1 Peter 5:6.

16. James 4:10 NKJV.

17. Matthew 11:29.

18. N. J. Opperwall, "Low; Lowly," in vol. 3 of *The International Standard Bible Encyclopedia*, rev. ed., ed. Geoffrey W. Bromiley (1915; repr., Eerdmans, 1979), 177.

19. Micah 6:8.

20. Psalm 10:12.

21. Psalm 10:17.

22. Psalm 25:9.

23. Psalm 9:10, 12 NKJV.

24. Psalm 149:4.

25. Proverbs 22:4.

26. Proverbs 3:34, 11:2.

27. Isaiah 29:19.

Lesson 6: Discover Genuine Happiness

1. Noah Agles, "How to Tell If Olive Tree Is Dead [and How to Revive It]," Garden Tabs, April 30, 2023, https://gardentabs.com/olive-tree-dead/.

2. Agles, "How to Tell If Olive Tree Is Dead"; "These Are the Oldest Olive Trees in the World," Finca Hermosa, accessed April 6,

2025, https://fincahermosa.com/hermosa/en/oldest-olive-trees
-the-world/.

3. "The Oldest Olive Tree in the World," Mia Elia, accessed
April 8, 2025, https://www.miaelia.com/the-oldest-olive
-tree-in-the-world/.

4. Damini R., "8 Oldest Olive Trees in History," Oldest.org,
March 20, 2025, https://www.oldest.org/nature/olive-trees/.

5. "These Are the Oldest Olive Trees in the World," Finca Hermosa.

6. Agles, "How to Tell If Olive Tree Is Dead."

7. Alejandra Borunda, "Italy's Olive Trees Are Dying. Can They
Be Saved?," *National Geographic*, accessed August 10, 2018,
https://www.nationalgeographic.com/science/article/italy
-olive-trees-dying-xylella.

8. Borunda, "Italy's Olive Trees Are Dying."

9. Psalm 52:8.

10. Allaya Cooks-Campbell, "Are You Languishing? Here's How
to Regain Your Sense of Purpose," BetterUp, October 27,
2021, https://www.betterup.com/blog/what-is-languish-how
-to-flourish.

11. Cooks-Campbell, "Are You Languishing?"; Maike Neuhaus,
"What Does It Mean to Languish?," *Psychology Today*,
December 1, 2021, https://www.psychologytoday.com/us/blog
/self-leadership/202112/what-does-it-mean-languish.

12. S. Fielding, "Feeling Blah During the Pandemic? It's Called
Languishing," *New York Times*, April 19, 2021, https://www
.nytimes.com/2021/04/19/well/mind/covid-mental-health
-languishing.html.

13. Cooks-Campbell, "Are You Languishing?"

14. Neuhaus, "What Does It Mean to Languish?"

15. Fielding, "Feeling Blah During the Pandemic?"

16. Cru Singapore, "Soul Anchors: From Languishing to
Flourishing," *Salt&Light*, October 22, 2021, https://saltandlight
.sg/devotional/soul-anchors-from-languishing-to-flourishing/.

17. Fielding, "Feeling Blah During the Pandemic?"

18. Psalm 6:2 ESV.
19. Jeremiah 31:25 AMPC.
20. John 11:25–26.
21. Romans 8:11.
22. Helena Rose Karnilowicz, "Flourishing: Definition, Aspects & Tips," Berkeley Well-Being Institute, accessed April 7, 2025, https://www.berkeleywellbeing.com/flourishing.html.
23. Michelle Flythe, "The Biology of Happiness," *Greater Good Magazine*, March 1, 2005, https://greatergood.berkeley.edu /article/item/the_biology_of_happiness.
24. "Happiness and Health," *Psychology Today*, accessed April 7, 2025, https://www.psychologytoday.com/us/basics/happiness /happiness-and-health.
25. Hebrews 13:8.
26. Matthew 19:26.
27. Psalm 128:2–3.

Lesson 7: Tap Into the Endless Oil of the Holy Spirit

1. "World Olive Oil Competition: 2025 Live Updates," *Olive Oil Times*, April 7, 2025, https://www.oliveoiltimes.com/live/world -olive-oil-competition-2025-live-updates/137353; Pablo Esparza, "In Slovenia, Hard Work and Keeping It Simple," *Olive Oil Times*, April 2, 2019, https://www.oliveoiltimes.com/world/in-slovenia -hard-work-and-keeping-it-simple/67519.
2. "Slovenian Olive Oil," Mediterannean, July 6, 2025, https:// enjoymediterranean.com/slovenian-olive-oil/.
3. Jerry James Stone, "History of Olives—What Am I Even Eating?!," *Jerry James Stone* (blog), November 26, 2023, https://jerryjamesstone.com/how-to/history-of-olives-what -am-i-even-eating/.
4. Leviticus 8:10–12; Psalm 133:2.
5. Genesis 28:16–18.
6. Exodus 40:9–16.
7. 1 Samuel 10:1.

Notes

8. 1 Samuel 16.
9. Zechariah 4:6.
10. Acts 10:38.
11. "What Does Christ Mean?," Bible Info, accessed April 17, 2025, https://www.bibleinfo.com/en/questions/what-does-christ-mean.
12. "What Does Christ Mean?," Bible Info; Matthew 16:16, 26:63; Luke 4:41.
13. Matthew 3:16; John 1:32.
14. Luke 4:18–19.
15. Anna Cooban and Xiaofei Xu, "The King's Coronation Brought in Far Fewer Viewers Than the Queen's Funeral," CNN, May 8, 2023, https://www.cnn.com/2023/05/08/media/coronation-viewing-figures/index.html.
16. Nedjeljko Jusup, "Consecrated Oil for King Charles III Coronation Arrives in London," *Olive Oil Times*, May 4, 2023, https://www.oliveoiltimes.com/business/europe/consecrated-oil-for-king-charles-iii-coronation-arrives-in-london/119406.
17. Meredith Faubel Nyberg, "Anointing," eds. John D. Barry et al., *The Lexham Bible Dictionary* (Lexham Press, 2016); Jack Hayford, "John 8–12: Jesus as the Anointed Prophet, Priest and King," Foursquare Church, December 14, 2012, https://resources.foursquare.org/jesus_as_the_anointed_prophet_priest_and_king/.
18. "The Consecration of the Coronation Oil," The Royal Family, March 3, 2023, https://www.royal.uk/news-and-activity/2023-03-03/the-consecration-of-the-coronation-oil.
19. Psalm 4:3.
20. Galatians 5:16.
21. John 15:26, 3:8; Romans 8:9, 15–16; Titus 3:5.
22. John 15:26.
23. Acts 2:2–4.
24. "Strong's #3875: Parakletos," Bible Tools, accessed April 8, 2025, https://www.bibletools.org/index.cfm/fuseaction/Lexicon.show/ID/G3875/parakletos.htm.

25. John 14:26 AMPC.
26. Philip Renner, "The Comforter, Part 1," Renner Ministries, accessed April 9, 2025, https://renner.org/article/the-comforter -part-1/; John 15:26; 16:7; 2 Corinthians 1:3.
27. Romans 8:13–16; Galatians 5:16–18.
28. John 16:13.
29. John 14:26.
30. Romans 8:26.
31. 1 Corinthians 2:12–14.

Lesson 8: Follow the Holy Spirit Your Guide

1. Aleksandrs Mozgovojs, "Seven Lakes Valley: A Gorgeous Full Day Hike in the Julian Alps," Sunset Obsession, August 8, 2022, https://sunsetobsession.com/seven-lakes-valley-hike/.
2. "Triglav National Park," National Parks, accessed April 8, 2025, https://national-parks.org/slovenia/triglav.
3. Merriam-Webster Dictionary, "Guide," accessed April 7, 2025, https://www.merriam-webster.com/dictionary/guide.
4. John 16:13.
5. Galatians 5:16.
6. John 14:17, 15:26.
7. John 6:44.
8. Isaiah 11:2.
9. Josh Tancordo, "Acts 16:6–15: The Ongoing Ministry of the Holy Spirit," Redeeming Grace Church, March 13, 2022, https://www .redeeminggracepittsburgh.com/sermons/sermon/2022-03-13 /acts-16:6-15:-the-ongoing-ministry-of-the-holy-spirit.
10. ESV.
11. Mark 16:20; Hebrews 2:4.
12. Exodus 20:14.
13. Malachi 3:6; Hebrews 13:8; Mark 12:30; Hebrews 10:23.
14. John 16:13, 14:26.
15. 1 Thessalonians 5:21.
16. Jeremiah 17:9.

Lesson 9: Seek Lasting Peace

1. UNHCR, "UN Refugee Agency Protection Chief Concludes Visit to Greece, Calling for Increased Protection for Refugees," July 28, 2023, https://www.unhcr.org/us/news/press-releases/un-refugee -agency-protection-chief-concludes-visit-greece-calling -increased.

2. "About UNHCR," UNHCR, accessed April 17, 2025, https:// www.unhcr.org/about-unhcr.

3. Genesis 5–9.

4. Genesis 8:3.

5. Genesis 8:1, 3.

6. Genesis 8:7.

7. Genesis 8:9.

8. Genesis 8:10–11.

9. Kashmira Gander, "Millennials Are the Most Anxious Generation, New Research Shows," *Newsweek*, May 9, 2018, https://www.newsweek.com/millennials-most-anxious -generation-new-research-shows-917095; Sue Shellenbarger, "The Most Anxious Generation Goes to Work," *Wall Street Journal*, May 9, 2019, https://www.wsj.com/articles/the-most -anxious-generation-goes-to-work-11557418951.

10. Gander, "Millennials Are the Most Anxious Generation"; Shellenbarger, "The Most Anxious Generation Goes to Work"; "Doom Scrolling and Its Effect on Your Mental Health," UNC Health Caldwell, May 16, 2023, https://www.caldwellmemorial .org/wellness/wellbeing-with-caldwell/doom-scrolling-and -its-effect-on-your-mental-health/.

11. "Doom Scrolling and Its Effect on Your Mental Health," UNC Health Caldwell.

12. Evan Starkman, "What's Doomscrolling and Can It Harm Me?," WebMD, November 6, 2024, https://www.webmd.com/balance /what-is-doomscrolling.

13. Jody Scott, "Why Millennials Are the Most Anxious Generation in History," *Vogue*, January 4, 2018, https://www.vogue.com.au

/beauty/wellbeing/why-millennials-are-the-most-anxious-generation-in-history/news-story/755e7b197bdb20c42b1c11d7f4 8525cd.

14. "Peace," King James Bible Dictionary, accessed April 7, 2025, https://kingjamesbibledictionary.com/Dictionary/peace.

15. Isaiah 9:6; John 14:27.

16. John 14:27.

17. Joshua M. Greever, "Peace," eds. John D. Barry et al., *The Lexham Bible Dictionary* (Lexham Press, 2016); 1 Samuel 20:7; Jeremiah 29:11, 38:4; Deuteronomy 23:6; Ezra 9:12; Jeremiah 33:9.

18. Kevin J. Timmer, "Shalom Seeking: Foundations of Flourishing," paper presented at the Christian Engineering Conference, Cedarville University, 2017, https://digitalcommons.cedarville .edu/cgi/viewcontent.cgi?article=1007&context=christian _engineering_conference.

19. *New Testament Greek Lexicon: New American Standard,* "Eirene Meaning," Bible Study Tools, accessed April 10, 2025, https:// www.biblestudytools.com/lexicons/greek/nas/eirene.html.

20. *New Testament Greek Lexicon,* "Eirene Meaning."

21. Galatians 5:22.

22. Colossians 3:15.

Lesson 10: Extend an Olive Branch

1. Galatians 5:22.

2. Rick Ezell, "Sermon: Being a Peacemaker—Matthew 5," Lifeway, January 1, 2014, https://www.lifeway.com/en/articles/sermon -blessed-peacemakers-sons-god-matthew-5.

3. Ezell, "Sermon: Being a Peacemaker."

4. "Enneagram Type 9: The Peacemaker," The Enneagram Institute, accessed April 10, 2025, https://www.enneagraminstitute.com /type-9/.

5. 2 Corinthians 5:18–19.

6. Philip Renner, "Making Wrongs Right," Renner Ministries,

accessed February 1, 2025, https://renner.org/article/making-wrongs-right/.

7. Erik Reed, "Do You Have to Reconcile in Order to Forgive?," Knowing Jesus Ministries, December 28, 2021, https://www.knowingjesusministries.co/articles/do-you-have-to-reconcile-in-order-to-forgive/.

8. Romans 12:18.

9. James 1:19–20.

10. Matthew 6:14–15.

11. Matthew 5:23–24.

Lesson 11: Disturb the Peace

1. "2022 Trafficking in Persons Report: Greece," US Department of State, accessed April 10, 2025, https://www.state.gov/reports/2022-trafficking-in-persons-report/greece/.

2. Acts 16:16–18.

3. "2022 Trafficking in Persons Report: Greece," US Department of State; Charalambos Kasimis, "Greece: Illegal Immigration in the Midst of Crisis," Migration Policy Institute, March 8, 2012, https://www.migrationpolicy.org/article/greece-illegal-immigration-midst-crisis.

4. Acts 10:38.

5. Luke 4:18–19.

6. Matthew 21:12–13; Isaiah 56:7–8; Jeremiah 7:11.

7. Jeffrey Curtis Poor, "What You Need to Know About Jesus Flipping Tables," Rethink, March 20, 2023, https://www.rethinknow.org/jesus-flipping-tables-matthew-21-12-13/.

8. "What Does It Mean That Jesus Overturns Tables (John 2:15)?," Got Questions, accessed April 9, 2025, https://www.gotquestions.org/Jesus-overturns-tables.html.

9. Molly S. Castelloe, "Dynamics of Emotional Contagion," Psychology Today, March 16, 2020, https://www.psychologytoday.com/us/blog/the-me-in-we/202003/dynamics-emotional-contagion; Douglas van Praet, "Emotional Contagion Drives

Social Media," *Psychology Today*, September 22, 2019, https://www.psychologytoday.com/us/blog/unconscious-branding/201909/emotional-contagion-drives-social-media.

10. Ephesians 4:15.
11. Isaiah 32:17.

Lesson 12: Produce Much Fruit

1. "Are Olives a Vegetable or Fruit?," Oliviers & Co., accessed April 7, 2025, https://oliviersandco.com/blog/olivesvegetable#.
2. "8 Amazing Attributes of Olive Trees That Will Humble and Inspire You," *Olive My Pickle*, accessed April 9, 2025, https://www.olivemypickle.com/blogs/news/8-amazing-attributes-of-olive-trees-that-will-humble-and-inspire-you.
3. Vangelis Kleft, "What Can Olive Pits Be Used For? Discover Their Full Potential," Oliviada, accessed April 8, 2025, https://www.oliviadaolive.com/what-can-olive-pits-be-used-for/.
4. "Every Fruit Mentioned in the Bible and Its Meaning," Tithe.ly, October 5, 2022, https://get.tithe.ly/blog/every-fruit-mentioned-in-the-bible-their-meaning.
5. John 15:8.
6. "Everything You Need to Know About Olive Varieties," *Brightland*, accessed April 9, 2025, https://brightland.co/blogs/field-notes/olive-varieties.
7. "Olive Sizes," Rada Olive, accessed April 9, 2025, https://www.radaolives.com/services/olive-sizes/.
8. Genesis 1:27; Psalm 139:14.
9. Luke 21:1–4.
10. Mark 5:19.
11. Chuck Broughton, "The Kingdom of God Is About Bearing Fruit," *Navigators*, October 1, 2013, https://www.navigators.org/blog/the-kingdom-of-god-is-about-bearing-fruit/.
12. John 5:4–5.
13. Matthew 6:33.
14. John 15:7.

15. John Piper, "What Does It Mean to 'Abide in Christ'?," Desiring God, September 22, 2017, https://www.desiringgod .org/interviews/what-does-it-mean-to-abide-in-christ.
16. Galatians 5:22–23.
17. Psalm 128:3.

Lesson 13: Accept the Pruning

1. Jason Frye, "Bosque el Olivar: Finding Peace in a City of 10 Million," *Travel Squire*, accessed April 9, 2025, https:// travelsquire.com/bosque-el-olivar/.
2. Colin Post, "Bosque el Olivar," Lima: City of Kings, May 7, 2018, http://limacitykings.com/bosque-el-olivar/.
3. Ann Fiorello Sievers, "Everybody, It Is Time to Prune the Olives and Do It Soon," Il Fiorello Olive Oil Company, March 2020, https://ilfiorello.com/everybody-it-is-time-to-prune-the-olives -and-do-it-soon/.
4. "First-Class Organic Food as a Result of Ecological Responsibility," Organic Farming Italy, accessed April 9, 2025, https://www.organicfarming-italy.info.
5. Debi Holland, "How to Prune Olive Trees—The Best Ways and When to Prune," *Homes & Gardens*, May 27, 2022, https://www .homesandgardens.com/gardens/how-to-prune-olive-trees.
6. Gilbert A. Smith, "How Do Trees Heal?," Arborsmith, April 2019, https://www.thearborsmiths.com/our-wisdom/how-do-trees -heal; Stephanie Rose, "Can Plants Feel Pain?," Garden Therapy, February 1, 2025, https://gardentherapy.ca/can-plants-feel-pain/.
7. John 15:1–2.
8. James Strong, *A Concise Dictionary of the Words in the Greek Testament and The Hebrew Bible* (Logos Bible Software, 2009), 38.
9. Psalm 103:13; 2 Corinthians 6:18; 2 Samuel 7:14; 1 Peter 5:7; Matthew 6:30–32.
10. Psalm 119:68.
11. John 15:2.

12. Matthew 12:46–50.
13. Jeremiah 23:16–22; Ezekiel 12:1–11.
14. Matthew 4:18–22; Mark 1:16–20.
15. Matthew 9:9; Luke 5:27–32.
16. Luke 8:1–9, 24:10; Mark 15:40–41; Matthew 27:55–56.
17. Philippians 3:8–9.
18. 1 Timothy 4:12.
19. "An Interview with Master Pruner Elizabeth Ruiz," Sloat Garden Center, February 3, 2025, https://sloatgardens.com/an-interview-with-master-pruner-elizabeth-ruiz/.
20. Galatians 5:22–23.
21. Psalm 92:13–14.

Lesson 14: Go Through the Press

1. Christine Caine, *How Did I Get Here? Finding Your Way Back to God When Everything Is Pulling You Away* (Thomas Nelson, 2021), 180–81.
2. "How to Harvest Olives," Olives Unlimited, accessed April 10, 2025, https://olivesunlimited.com/how-to-harvest-olives/.
3. David Wise, "The Oil Press of Gethsemane," March to Zion, February 19, 2021, https://marchtozion.com/the-oil-press-of-gethsemane/.
4. Luke 22:44.
5. 2 Corinthians 5:21.
6. Luke 22:42.
7. *Strong's Greek Lexicon*, "1014: boulomai," Bible Hub, accessed April 17, 2025, https://biblehub.com/greek/1014.htm; *Strong's Greek Lexicon*, "2307: theléma," Bible Hub, accessed April 17, 2025, https://biblehub.com/greek/2307.htm.
8. Galatians 5:16–17.
9. Romans 8:28.
10. John 10:10.
11. Isaiah 55:8–9.
12. Proverbs 3:5–6.

13. Mark 14:36.
14. Hebrews 13:8–16.
15. Matthew 16:24.
16. 2 Timothy 4:7.

Epilogue: The Olive Tree, an Enduring Evergreen

1. "Chinese Olives," Specialty Produce, accessed April 10, 2025, https://specialtyproduce.com/produce/Chinese_Olives_8482.php.
2. "Chinese Olives," Specialty Produce.
3. Mac Wiener, "The Spiritual Significance of Trees," Banner, April 13, 2020, https://www.thebanner.org/features/2020/04/the-spiritual-significance-of-trees.
4. Tree and Landscape Board, "The Benefits of Evergreens," *City of College Park Municipal Scene*, PDF, 10, https://www.collegeparkmd.gov/DocumentCenter/View/6548/Municipal-Scene---January-2024.
5. Jeremiah 17:7–8.
6. Isaiah 41:19 NIV.
7. "Isaiah 41:19 Commentaries," Bible Hub, accessed April 10, 2025, https://biblehub.com/commentaries/isaiah/41-19.htm.
8. "God's Trail of Trees," Plant with Purpose, February 5, 2019, https://plantwithpurpose.org/trailoftrees/.
9. John Stonestreet and G. Shane Morris, "Why God Uses Trees as a Metaphor," *Christian Today*, May 28, 2019, https://christiantoday.com/article/why-god-uses-trees-as-a-metaphor/132526.htm.
10. Wiener, "Spiritual Significance of Trees"; "Humans Are . . . Trees?," episode 1 of *Tree of Life*, produced by Tim Mackie and Jon Collins, podcast, 1:07:02, Bible Project, January 6, 2020, https://bibleproject.com/podcast/humans-are-trees/.
11. "Olive Trees," Bible Places, accessed April 10, 2025, https://www.bibleplaces.com/olive-trees.
12. Jeremiah 11:16.
13. Hebrews 12:27.

14. Isaiah 55:13 NET.

About the Author

Christine Caine is a speaker, activist, and bestselling author who awakens people globally to discover their God-given purpose and live transformed lives for Jesus.

Christine and her husband, Nick, have two daughters, Catherine and Sophia. Together they founded A21, a global anti-human trafficking organization that prevents exploitation, recovers victims, and empowers survivors to rebuild their lives. She also founded Propel Women, an initiative that activates women to follow Jesus wholeheartedly and live confidently in their God-given purpose. You can tune into Christine's *Equip & Empower* podcast and *Life & Leadership* podcast for practical insights and encouragement, drawing hope from Jesus wherever you are. To learn more about Christine and her resources, visit www.christinecaine.com.